Pray as You Go

Pray as You Go

ON LIVING YOUR FAITH
IN THE NINETIES

By Dr. Robert Meneilly

Andrews and McMeel
A Universal Press Syndicate Company
Kansas City

Pray as You Go: On Living Your Faith in the Nineties
copyright © 1996 by Robert Meneilly.
Andrews and McMeel, a Universal Press Syndicate Company,
4520 Main Street, Kansas City, Missouri 64111.

Library of Congress Cataloging-in-Publication Data

Meneilly, Robert.
Pray as you go : on living your faith in
the nineties /Robert Meneilly.
p.   cm.
ISBN 0-8362-2170-2 (hardbound)
1. Spiritual life—Christianity. 2. Christian life. 3. Faith.
4. Prayer—Christianity. I. Title.
BV 4501.2.M447 1966
248.4—dc20   96-26848
CIP

This book

is dedicated to

my beloved wife,

Shirley,

for almost fifty years

my partner in all things,

and the

Village Presbyterian Church family,

who nurtured us with love

and encouragement

for forty-eight years.

Contents

Contents

Acknowledgments

Our son, Rob, has been the prime mover of this book. He was rather insistent that I share some of my meditations and thoughts with a larger audience. He has shared in this publication with his own art style as well as his encouragement.

I am grateful for the staff of Andrews and McMeel, who have contributed the skills I do not possess to make this publication possible.

1

How to Stay Alive as Long as You Live

*F*or many people, living seems to be one continuous headache. They may seem to have everything, but they have little life. Scores of these people, up-and-outers as much as down-and-outers, know little real enjoyment and only rare moments of good laughter. So many of them look strained. They feel everything is against them; nothing goes right. They are commonly heard to say, "If it isn't one thing, it's another." So they take two more Excedrin to dull the pain and drag themselves into the necessary survival exercises for the day.

Lots of people still physically alive are spiritually dead. More of them than you would imagine harbor a secret death wish much of the time—this is just as true of teenagers as it is of older people. They have died years ahead of the time when a physician pronounces them dead. Actually, relatively few people get as much life into their years or years into their life as God intends. Researchers tell us we all abbreviate our life span by an average of fifteen years by our failure to manage day-to-day stress and worry. Instead of doing something constructive about what is bothering us and exercising our God-given faith, we allow anxiety and distress to wear us down.

God tells us, "I have set before you life and death, . . . choose life so that you . . . may live." Scripture goes on to explain that real living is "loving the Lord your God, obeying him, and holding fast to him; for that means life to you" (Deut. 30:19–20).

God's word has one message from beginning to end: life. God creates us after his own likeness and breathes his life into us. We destroy the quality of that life by ignoring God's laws and trying to play God ourselves. In spite of our sin, God keeps coming with all the love he ever had for us. If we respond to his love, accepting Jesus Christ as our Savior, we die with Christ to sin and, with him, come alive to God again (see Rom. 6:5–11). Jesus made the claim, "I am the life"(John 14:6). If we want to find real life, we find it in Christ. As the apostle Paul said, "For me to live is Christ"(Phil. 1:21).

This is what is meant by "being born again, born from above." The person who takes Jesus Christ into his or her heart becomes a whole new creation. Just as we are born of our earthly parents and resemble them, the believer is reborn of our heavenly Parent and resembles our Parent from above. A well-known clergyman of the nineteenth century, Dwight L. Moody, said: "What is born of the flesh dies; what is born of the Spirit lives forever." Jesus Christ gives to everyone who receives him a new lease on real life.

All this gives us, as Christians, serious reason to learn how to live life and stay alive as long as we live. We need to learn how to take this new life in Christ and live it up. How do we get more quality life into our given years? How do we get more mileage out of our human energy?

We need to get our heads together with God's. A busy man came home from work late one evening. Hearing his footsteps, his son called him into his room. The boy asked, "Dad, is it true two heads are better than one?" "I guess they are," the father replied. To this the boy said, "Then why doesn't your head help my head with these homework problems?"

That youngster was no dummy. What if you put your head together with God's mind to work on your problems? The Bible tells us to get our head together with God's and think: "Whatever is true ... honorable ... just ... pure ... pleasing ... commendable ... think about these things" (Phil. 4:8). The Bible also bids us, "Let the same mind be in you that was also in Christ Jesus" (Phil. 2:5).

How we use our mind and draw upon the mind of God determines the quality of our life and, perhaps, even the quantity of our life. Our happiness or unhappiness is very much the product of our thinking. As the proverb puts it, "As a person thinks in the heart, so is that person."

How we think of God shapes our spiritual life. How we think of ourselves is the script we follow as we live. How we think of people determines how we love or hate. How we think of any event determines how we evaluate that happening, which in turn determines how we feel about it.

A man was wounded by a gunshot. People around him were sure the bullet had passed through his body. Hearing this, the man fainted and fell to the ground as if dead. He was rushed to the hospital. On the table in the emergency room, he was found to have little more than a shallow flesh wound. Hearing this, the man got up, smiled, and left as if nothing had happened. How and what we believe about ourselves determines how we feel.

Most of us never begin to tap the power of our mind. God has placed all kinds of resources for health and the good life within us. Physicians report that many of their patients have nothing wrong with them except their thoughts. In this day of dependency on miracle drugs, more people look to outside help and neglect the built-in health resources God has provided. One noted physician is reported to write out this prescription for many of his patients: "Be transformed by the renewing of your mind" (Rom. 12:2).

Many of us could enjoy far better health, lots more happiness, and much greater self-control if we would change our way of thinking. Try to think of any given situation as you believe Christ would think of it. Put your head together with God's. God has put something miraculous within our mind that, when joined with the mind of Christ, can brace us for any crisis, set the natural built-in healing processes of our body to work, and make us more than equal to any need or emergency.

There is a heap of wisdom in the song from *The King and I*, "Whenever I feel afraid . . . I whistle a happy tune." The power of the mind over the body is more powerful than any miracle drug.

Talking about miracle drugs, the most effective drug I know is the Twenty-third Psalm. I have seen many persons—sick, troubled, anxious, or frightened—keep repeating that psalm. They think God's thoughts after him until they have his mind working with their mind, and then they come through with flying colors.

How well and how much we live day by day depends on the extent to which we allow ourselves to be saturated with God's teachings. The degree to which we have the mind of Christ determines whether we succeed or fail, are strong or weak, confident or frightened, healthy or sickly. Remember, it is having the mind of Christ that is important. The psalmist claims that the person who relies upon his or her own mind alone is a fool. The secret of living is getting our head together with God.

Many people never enjoy life before their body dies only because of their procrastination. We have a habit of putting good things off. Felix was appointed procurator of Judea by the emperor. He was married to a beautiful Jewish woman, whom he had seduced from her lawful husband. He ordered the apostle Paul brought from his prison cell because he wanted to hear him preach. Paul preached before the procurator and his wife, Drusilla, about one's personal faith in Jesus Christ (Acts 24). He also spoke so persuasively about justice, self-control, and judgment that Felix trembled. But when Felix was almost convinced to adopt the new life in Christ, he dismissed Paul, saying he would have him back when he got the chance. He was on the threshold of abundant living, the good life, peace with God, and hope beyond this present life, but he put it off. Felix died before he lived, a victim of his own procrastination. How often this story is repeated among us!

Tomorrow, and tomorrow, and tomorrow,
Creeps in this petty pace from day to day,
To the last syllable of recorded time;
And all our yesterdays have lighted fools
The way to dusty death.

Shakespeare, *Macbeth*

On the tombstone of a New England youth are these words: *This I expected, but not so soon.* So many people die before they live, because they never quite got around to taking Jesus Christ seriously to heart.

Job asked the question, "Is there life after death?" The question should be, "Is there life after birth?" We dare not put God off. He is saying to us, "Now is the acceptable time; see, now is the day of salvation!" (2 Cor. 6:2).

To be full of life, be full of joy. We are as happy as we make up our mind to be; we are as unhappy as we make up our mind to be. Many people are dead on the vine because they are unhappy. Happy thinking is essential to well-being.

We see on television how coaches cheer on their athletes. Coaches know the importance of joy in readying contenders. Joy lubricates the mind, the nerves, the muscles, and the heart.

We all know what it takes to live a joyful life. Quit hating people and start loving them—even enemies. Quit being angry with people and start forgiving them. Quit doing wrong and start doing right. Quit thinking only about yourself and go out and do something for others. We all know what things we have to do to be happy, but we don't get around to doing them. Jesus said, "If you know these things, you are blessed if you do them" (John 13:17).

Have you not observed this law of life: "The proportion to which you give joy, you receive joy"? It is the law of reciprocity. Joy increases as you give it and diminishes as you try to keep it for yourself. Think joy. Talk joy. Practice joy. Saturate your mind with joy, and you will have the time of your life all your life. It will also cause you to stay alive as long as you live.

Many people, as they grow old, cease to live very much. Some let themselves be crushed by broken dreams. Some allow repeated disappointments to make them cynical. Some are frightened by the aging process. Some retire unprepared and, feeling useless, spend what could be their best years dying a slow death.

Worshiping at the shrine of youth seems to be an American psychosis. However, those really alive want to be exactly the age they are, because this is the context in which God has put them. Those who would live as long as they have life learn to shift gears according to the climb.

The psalmist prayed, "So teach us to count our days that we may gain a wise heart" (Ps. 90:12). Prize every present day. Keep an open heart and an open mind. Be willing to consider new thoughts, new ideas, and learn new things.

Think of old age as the prelude to eternal life with God. It was written of Enoch that he walked with God and never tasted death (Heb. 11:5). A Sunday school youngster, asked to tell what she thought that meant, explained, "Every day God and Enoch took long walks together. One day Enoch became very tired, and God invited him into his house to rest for as long as he wanted to stay."

Walking close to God, hand in hand with Christ, one moves gracefully into age and maturity. It is said that the closer we come to the sunset of earth, the closer is the sunrise of heaven.

To stay alive all your life, pray as you go. Pray your way all the way. Pray at all times, and at all times you will know that you are in God's presence and care. Prayer will bring your head and God's head together. God is your data base for wisdom. He is always cheering you on. He is the very strength of your life. Hold on to God as he holds you, and you will live as long as God has life!

Jesus said, "I am the resurrection and the life. Those who believe in me, even though they die, will live; and everyone who lives and believes in me will never die" (John 11:25). And an old Quaker is reported to have said, "I am going to live until I die, and then I am going to live all over again." How is it with you?

2

Where There's Hope,
There's Life

Around emergency rooms and intensive care units of hospitals, one hears it echoed to anxious families gathered in the waiting rooms, "Where there's life, there's hope." It suggests that as long as the patient is hanging on, there is hope he or she will come through. I have always felt that such an expression should be turned around. "Where there's hope, there's life." Legitimate hope is what sustains life.

The story is told that, years ago, a submarine was rammed by another ship and quickly sank. The crew was trapped in a prison house of death. Other ships rushed to the scene of the disaster, just off the coast of Massachusetts. Not much is known of what took place down in the sunken and disabled submarine, but we can imagine how frantic the men must have become as the oxygen slowly ran out. Pressing his helmeted ear to the side of the vessel, a diver heard a tapping sound. Someone inside was tapping out a question in the dots and dashes of Morse Code. The question came slowly: "Is . . . there . . . any . . . hope?"

A person in mid-life, stricken with a crippling disease affecting the nervous system and muscles, facing a future wheelchair-to-bed existence, cries out within, "Is there any hope?"

A marriage becomes impossible. Counseling has been to no avail. Both partners will lose in a divorce, to say nothing of what it will mean to the children. Life is miserable for everyone in the household, and even the children wonder, "Is there any hope?"

An aging man, suffering from deterioration of the body and needing special care, remains at home. With two sons disputing what he should do, and with little prospect of improving his condition, his soul cries out, "Is there any hope?"

Older folks, reminiscing about better times, look at the changes in our present society through the glasses of the good old days and see the deterioration of the modern family—new epidemics like AIDS, the crisis of health care, illegal aliens overrunning communities, violence everywhere, governments no longer able to solve social problems—and they ask, "Is there any hope?"

Folks in the urban ghetto, seeing one person after another taken down by shootings and violence—with disruptive drug houses on the streets where they must live and unemployed adults hanging around the street corners—and finding themselves locked into an imprisoning environment from which they cannot escape, cry out, "Is there any hope?"

Hope is the very essence of human life. The Bible reminds us that where there is no hope, a people will perish. Only men and women created in the image of God have hope. No other animal life depends on hope. Hope has to do with the future, and only human beings have real concern for the future. It is natural for us to think about the future, because we are going to spend the rest of our lives there! Without hope, we would live only for the present— eat, drink, and be merry, for tomorrow we die. But God has put eternity in the minds of humans (Eccl. 3:11). The God-given hope we have for the future shapes all our attitudes and determines our present living.

While faith and hope are two sides of the same coin, faith is based on past performance, while hope is anticipation of the future. History bears much influence on our present hope. Because of our faith in God, who has acted consistently throughout history to save his people, we have every reason to be positive about the future. We all know that yesterday's experiences affect today's hope. It is said that today, well lived, makes every tomorrow a vision of hope. At the same time, today poorly lived makes tomorrow hopeless.

Without hope, we cannot survive. We survive the problems, pains, and sorrows of the present, and even mature from them, because hope always lives in the future. The parent can tolerate, and often enjoy, the cost and stress of parenting because the parent is able to picture a good, responsible citizen in future years. A person can face surgery and painful physical therapy with the hope of comfort and wholeness ahead. A student can endure the discipline and stress of tough courses and exams, because he or she looks forward to the day when it can all be put to practical use in making a living. Samuel Johnson observed, "Where there is no hope, there can be no endeavor."

The most pitiful person is the one who has no hope. The patient who loses all hope of feeling better usually never will feel better. The person who loses hope that society will ever be any better usually does nothing to make it better. The person who loses hope of the magnificent future God has planned for us won't appreciate the grace of God that is sufficient for the present and will slip into a pit of depression. The apostle Paul wrote, "If for this life only we have hoped in Christ, we are of all people most to be pitied" (1 Cor. 15:19).

Some people tend to rev up false hopes—optimists to a fault. They are dreamers, not realists. How many Americans keep hoping to win the Powerball lottery and dream of the things they will do with all that money! There are individuals who put all their hope on a particular person, only to have that person let them down. There are others who put all their hope on their own skills, ingenuity, and hard work, only to become incapacitated when their physical health breaks down. Some put their hope on their investments, and the bottom drops out of the market. False hopes lead us in wrong ways and bring us to wrong ends.

It is not a generic kind of hope of which we write. Usually, hoping refers to a vague sort of future expectation. People hope for something they want very much to happen, or something that would be a desirable solution to a serious problem they are facing. There is no assurance that things will turn out as they would like, but they have "high hopes."

Unlike that uncertain hope, Christian hope is based on the assurance that comes from faith in God. Anyone may dream of better things to come, but the Christian bases hope not on some future happening but on the fact that God has already given the sure ground of hope in Jesus Christ. Hope in God is the only authentic hope! Accept no substitutes!

The Bible bids us to "seize the hope set before us. We have this hope, a sure and steadfast anchor of the soul" (Heb. 6:18–19). In a very troubled world, hope must have a guarantee. Without such grounds in God, our world would be overwhelmed by despair.

The Bible also reminds us, "Now hope that is seen is not hope. For who hopes for what is seen?" (Rom. 8:24). Our future is not now in hand. We cannot see it, but it is not unknown. God knows it and has everything in hand.

The hope that Christianity brings is not a Pollyanna lift, unrealistic positive thinking, or lighthearted spirits. It is a sure conviction that God does have everything in hand, and that what is best for us will ultimately be accomplished because nothing can thwart our sovereign God's will. The person who loses hope loses life. It has been suggested that hope is the nerve and the muscle of everything we endeavor. Doubt is debilitating; hope is energizing.

No one suffers more than the person who is without hope in God. The wounded wife, who has lost her husband through divorce and has no hope of a better tomorrow, dies a bit every day. The man whose wife has died, and who can see no hope of ever being happy again, suffers by the hour. The student who has no hope of making it through school, and no dreams for the future, has no drive to do what is at hand to assure a better tomorrow. The person who has terminal cancer, and no hope in God and God's promise of heaven, abhors the thought of dying. Clinical depression is described as "a feeling of utter hopelessness."

So many people are dying for want of hope in God. Some see nothing but a dismal future for our economy, our government, our public schools, our families, and our institutions. They are skeptical, pessimistic, and cynical. They are spiritually dead, though clinically alive.

To live we must have hope in God. We can be sure the future will bring us our share of trials and troubles, but with God-given hope we can believe God's word when we read, "We triumph even in our sufferings, knowing that suffering produces endurance, and endurance produces character, and character produces hope, and hope does not disappoint us" (Rom. 5:3–5).

I don't know who it was who suggested that hope in God is applying our future security to our present problems. Every day we are saved from all kinds of things by hope in God. Because of God's consistent and faithful past performance, we know the tide will come back in; dawn will come with the morning; this trouble, too, shall pass; and weariness will give way to joy.

The person who has the God-given hope that goes beyond this present life is the person who is trustworthy, tenacious, and responsible, makes time count, and enjoys life with all of its ups and downs. The person who has no hope for the next world does nothing for this present one.

The old saying is true. "Life with Christ is an endless hope; without him, a hopeless end." There is never such a thing as a hopeless situation; there are only persons who lose their hope. If you want to get lots more life out of living, live under this benediction: "May the God of hope fill you with all joy" (Rom. 15:13).

3

Failing Isn't Fatal

*D*o you feel that you are a failure in some area of your life? You are not alone. Anyone who has the nerve to do anything will fail at times.

There is nothing fatal about failing. Even to fail at many things is not a sign that you are a failure. If you are failing often it is only a sign that you are often trying. Better to have tried and failed than never to have tried at all.

Failure is very often the seed to success, a blessing in disguise. Failure opens the door to both knowledge and wisdom through the trial-and-error method. Failure may open the door to faith and patience. Failure reveals the things that won't work. Failure cures vain persons of conceit. When you are discouraged with feelings of failure, remember no failure is final. It may be the prelude to genuine success.

Do you know why the Christian faith is always spoken of as "good news"? The Christian life is a whole lifetime of fresh starts. It is the religion of the second chance, and not just a second chance but an infinite number of chances. After all, the cardinal truth of this faith—the resurrection—began with the failure of a civil judicial system and a murder!

No failure is final until we accept it as such. Failure is a figment of the imagination, but imagined failure is just as damaging as real failure.

A fifth grader gets a bad grade on several tests. It is implied by the grade, the teacher, and the parents that the boy is a failure. Accepting himself as a failure, there is a good chance that he will continue to fail. It has been demonstrated that children in a system of education that does not allow them to experience success in school live out their lives as social failures. Failure breeds failure if persons think they are losers. A taste of success breeds success. No youngster is a failure until he or she is convinced of it by outsiders and buys into that falsehood.

A young woman fails to make it in one college and then another, at one job and several successive jobs. Society, and even family by innuendo, communicates to her, "You are a disappointment, a failure. You are never going to make it." The question is, "Make what?" Such a person, convinced that she is a failure, keeps on setting herself up for failure to remain true to her self-image.

A mother worries about her prodigal child who goes off into the far country of wild living. She questions her parenting. "Where did I go wrong? How could I have failed so?" The mother may cry, as if her entire life is one super-failure, without ever enjoying the other ninety-nine achievements of her life.

It is the law of human nature that we always act according to what we believe or imagine to be true about ourselves and our environment. If we picture ourselves as failures, we will act in failing ways.

As a young lad, the famed psychologist Alfred Adler was not doing well in math class. A parent-teacher conference was called, with both teacher and parents now convinced the boy was a dummy in math. It did not take long for the student to believe it. Adler did poorly, acting out what he believed to be true about himself.

Failing at something is a blessing or a curse, depending on one's reaction to it. If we respond to failure as a nudge from the Spirit of God, who is at work within us, to turn around and do a thing differently, the experience is almost sure to prove a blessing. If we accept the failure as a sign of weakness, and brood over it until it becomes an inferiority complex, it will be a curse.

No one who is doing anything worthwhile has immunity against failing. The saintliest saints are as subject to failing as anyone else. Everyone fails many times during a lifetime. How we respond to a given failure determines whether it will be a blessing or a curse, the making of us or the breaking of us. Failure affects people in one of two ways: It serves as a challenge to greater effort or a discouragement that leads to giving up. Take a look at how you respond to failure, and you can tell if you are a potential achiever or a quitter.

Many of today's failures will be tomorrow's heroes. Most failures are only temporary defeats that can be converted into priceless assets, if we trust ourselves to God and do our very best. People are usually generous in forgiving our failures, providing we accept them as such and keep on trying, but the world is slow to forgive those who quit when the going gets tough.

People still celebrate Babe Ruth as baseball's classic hero. But do you know that Babe Ruth struck out more than any other player in baseball history? He failed at least 1,330 times at bat to get to first base. It didn't frustrate him to strike out. The fellow who first discovered Babe Ruth is reported to have said that Babe Ruth looked better striking out than when hitting a home run! When Babe struck out, he never counted it a failure; it was an effort! Once asked what he did when he got into a batting slump, the Babe replied, "I just keep goin' up there and swinging at 'em. I know the old law of averages will hold good for me, the same as it does for anybody else, if I keep havin' my healthy swings. If I strike out two or three times in a game or fail to get a hit for a week, why should I worry? Let the pitchers worry; they're the guys who're gonna suffer later on."

Lincoln may have been America's number-one loser. He did not even make it to first base in his bid for the Illinois legislature. He failed as a storekeeper and was seventeen years paying off his debts. He was badly beaten in his bid for Congress. He was anything but a success in his law practice. He didn't make it as a surveyor. He failed as a soldier. He even failed when he tried to get an appointment to the U.S. Land Office. These were all miserable disappointments, but he kept on trying, and he became the greatest hero in American history. President Lincoln is reported to have said, "My great concern is not whether you have failed but whether you are content with your failure."

Thomas Edison was a habitual failure. His teacher sent him home from school with a note saying he would never make it as a student. He had more than ten thousand failures before he invented the incandescent bulb. He believed that each failure brought him that much closer to success. His failings opened the door to all kinds of inventions he would never have made otherwise.

We all fail repeatedly. Who of us doesn't fail to live up to what God created us to be? We have temptations we fail to resist. We have good intentions we fail to implement. What we should do, we fail to do; what we ought not to do, we succeed in doing. Some of us become so discouraged trying to live the Christian life because of repeated failings, we drift away from the church and give up. Others take each failure as a signal to turn to Christ, change direction, and try again. The saint is simply a forgiven sinner who keeps on trying.

At whatever we fail, we must remember God's unfailing presence. If God is present, every experience is useful. God works even our failures together for our ultimate good if we love him and try to live according to his purpose.

Consider the apostle Peter. Jesus picked him up when he was little more than a rough-and-tough fisherman and Jesus made him into a real man. He asked nothing more of him than his faithfulness. Peter promised, but look what happened! As soon as Jesus was taken, Peter failed him by whacking off the arresting officer's ear. Only a few hours later, he denied Jesus three times over. Only when Jesus asked him three times, "Peter, do you love me?" did Peter realize how he had failed. His failure is what moved him to renew his commitment to Christ. His life may have looked as if it failed when he died upside down on a cross because of his undying commitment to his Lord, but it was a failing that made for success; for the only ultimate success on earth or in heaven is faithfulness to the Highest.

God converts failures into successes as long as there is faithfulness and trying. God converted the failure symbolized in the cross to the success of Christ's (and our own) resurrection and the redemption of the world.

One of the most unfortunate things in our communities is that we only train our children for success; seldom do we train them to handle failure. Yet what is success? The *American Heritage Dictionary* defines it as "the achievement of something desired, planned or attempted." Then the dictionary adds a quote from Emily Dickinson: "Success is counted sweetest by those who ne'er succeed."

What the world calls success may not be all that wonderful. We all know people, very successful in the eyes of the world at making a living, who are miserable failures at making a life.

Several years ago Abingdon Press published a book, *Success Is Failure Experience*, written by William L. Malcomson. The book deals with the success syndrome. Some people climb over others to achieve their goals. Is that success? Americans conform to the secular myths of success and do whatever it requires, even to trade their souls for it. Such success is a failure experience.

Malcomson takes up the so-called success in religion. He writes about the difference between American religion and the Christian gospel. American religion holds to the myth of success, which says if something is successful it must be right, because it would not succeed without God's favor.

It is amazing how many contemporary Christians hold to the Deuteronomic view of history: If you do right, you will be rewarded with God's goodies; if you do wrong, you will be punished. If things are going well with you, God is looking after you (blessing you). If things are going poorly, we are being tested by God or we would have goofed. If we are successful at our religion—enjoy praying every day; have "joy, joy, joy" down in our hearts; appear radiant and have perfect peace of mind—we must be OK. God must be on our side. Religious success may be no more than spiritual morphine to which religionists become addicted.

Religious success makes for holier-than-thous in our eyes and total failures in God's sight.

Jesus calls us beyond what the world calls success. He calls us to measure life by a standard greater than all others, which is called "faithfulness." The person dedicated to being faithful to his or her Lord and to life's highest calling (God's purpose) will find in every failure God's urging to ultimate achievement—faithfulness. Every failure tells us something is wrong so we can learn what is right. Discovery is born in failures. It is in my repeated failings that I discover God and a better way. There are no creations without experiments.

Allow yourself to believe that you are a failure and you will succeed in failing. Believe yourself born of God, born to win, and a winner you will be. Your failings are calling you to be faithful. Be diligently faithful to God and leave any success to Him.

So you have been afraid that you are a failure? Take heart and be of good cheer. Your failures are your assets in God's making.

4

Pray as You Go

If you want to get more life out of living and more mileage out of your life, learn to pray as you go. When you are not praying much, you don't go far!

God is always in touch with us, whether we are aware of that fact or not. The question is whether we are in touch with God. God has made prayer the way to his presence. In that sneak preview of heaven given John, the risen living Christ is pictured as knocking at the door of our hearts and patiently waiting for us to open up to him (Rev. 3:20). Prayer is the opening of the door to let Christ in.

We may think of God's presence as operating something like atmospheric pressure, equally present everywhere. Augustine found that God was as present in the pub as in the church. The scripture bids us to "call upon him while he is near." While God is always everywhere near, his presence is realized only by those who pray.

By not praying and keeping in close touch with God, we miss receiving all the good things our Heavenly Father wants to give us. Nothing is received from God except by prayer. Many persons wallow in spiritual poverty, surrounded by all the riches of God, only because they do not pray.

Sometimes we don't pray because we don't think ourselves worthy of expecting anything from God. God loves the sinner as much as the saint. You can be sure that prayer is for everyone, not for a select few.

Some Christians will pray but do little more than pray. They substitute prayer for good works and productivity. If our prayer does not result in productivity for God, it is fraud. Prayer is actually working God's will with God's strength.

Some people pray as a means of avoiding hard reality. They hide out in the ether waves of spirituality and never touch the ground of reality. It is like the "positive thinking" freaks who look at everything so positively that they never do anything about negative things. Such pray-ers just pass everything over to God and evade their own responsibility. We have no right to push over onto God what God is equipping us and expecting us to do for ourselves. Prayer can be used as a crutch, rather than a ladder, but prayer used as a crutch will never get us off the ground!

Some pray in an unconscious attempt to use God as a means toward their own ends rather than letting God use them as a means toward his ends. Too much of our praying is self-centered rather than God-centered.

Prayer may be likened to a radio receiver. God is always attempting to speak to us, but it is only when we have our prayer receiver turned on that we can hear him. Prayer is even better than a radio because it is two-way communication. Too frequently, our prayers are only one way. We do all the talking and never extend to God the courtesy to get in a word.

Often our praying is telling God what he should do, when we should be reporting to God for duty. We need to be up and doing what we pray. Jesus never tried to tell the Father what to do. He prayed so the Father could show him what *he* was to do. Would that we learn to let God supervise us rather than trying to supervise the Almighty!

I got a new perspective on prayer by reading in an old book about an early church father who said that prayer is "the breath of the soul." Prayer is to the soul what breathing is to the lungs. As much as we must keep breathing to stay physically alive, so we must keep praying to stay spiritually alive. Even as the respiratory system must be kept working to keep the body alive, so our prayer system must be kept working to keep our soul alive. We do not take a few deep breaths in the morning, let the lungs be at rest, and then take a few more deep breaths before we go to sleep to get through the night. We breathe all day long when awake and all night long while asleep, continuously taking in oxygen to combust our food fuel, to turn it into usable energy, and exhaling the poison of carbon dioxide to keep cleansing our system. By praying "without ceasing," we keep inhaling the life-giving breath of God, which gives us spiritual energy, and exhaling the waste products of sin, frustration, worry, and fear.

If we don't keep breathing through our lungs as we go, we don't go far. If we don't pray as we go, we won't go far. The scripture calls upon us to be praying at all times and in all places. We are to make our life one unceasing prayer.

There are times when we feel weak and anxious, less than able to handle what is on our mind. We wonder why. Probably it is because we are not letting our soul breathe. No spiritual oxygen is being taken in to combust the faith fuel that God has given us. No matter how great that fuel, it cannot be converted into usable energy without the spiritual oxygen of God's energizing breath. What is the matter with most of us much of the time is that our souls are suffocating to death. We hold our spiritual breath and then wonder why we suffer the blues.

Read again the creation story in Genesis and see how God gave us life like his own in the first place. God breathed his own Spirit-breath into animal life, and man and woman became live human beings in God's likeness. Only praying as we go keeps that same life-giving Spirit-breath of God coming into us so we stay alive and well.

Someone once spoke of prayer as the pulse of a renewed soul, whose constant beat is the test and measure of one's spiritual life. The physician checks our pulse to discern the condition of our physical heart. Check your prayer pulse, and you can diagnose the condition of your spiritual heart. Too often we find more hardening of the arteries than hardening of the knee joints from kneeling in prayer. When the nurse or physician can find no pulse beat, the patient is pronounced dead. Take your own prayer pulse.

We need to remember that the most important thing in any prayer is not what or how we say something to God but in hearing what God has to say to us. Prayer should be more our listening than our talking. Jesus counsels us, "Do not heap up empty phrases as the Gentiles do; for they think that they will be heard because of their many words" (Matt. 6:7).

An infant in the crib cannot say, "I need a new Huggie," or "I'm starving," or "I have a bad stomachache." All the child can do is scream. The parent hears the cry and responds to the need. Any good parent understands the cry of a helpless child and answers. As a parent cares for a child, so will God take care of you.

Perhaps our best prayers are prayed when we are not even conscious that we are praying. The Bible tells us that God's Spirit is within each of us, praying for us—"sighs too deep for words" (Rom. 8:26). With our more formal prayers, our real prayer may come only after we have said "Amen." Those who pray as they ought will strive to live as they pray.

We are what we pray. We are only as alive as our prayers. Our daily life is only as limited as our daily prayers. God is never farther away than our prayers.

If we have any real care for God, we will give him the time of day. Prayer is taking time out to take God in. If prayer is a matter of hit-and-miss, there will be more misses than hits in our life. As the Christian grows in faith, praying becomes the Christian's lifestyle.

Prayer is doing our best and then trusting God to do the rest. The Germans have a proverb: "Pray as though no work would help, and work as if no prayer would help."

Prayer is the receptacle by which we receive from God what he wants to give us. We have not from God only because we pray not.

Prayer is the source of God's power for our life. It is like turning on a light switch. It does not create the electric current; it simply provides the channel through which the current may flow. Keep praying, and you keep tapping the power of God. When we don't "turn on," the power of God doesn't come through.

Let it be understood that prayer must first move the person who prays. God doesn't wait to be moved by our feeble prayers. Prayer doesn't change God. In fact, prayer doesn't change any circumstance. Prayer changes the person who prays, and then God uses a changed person to change things.

We are assured in scripture that God answers every prayer. When I first began to feel the pain of separation from my church family of forty-seven years, I shamefully confess that I asked God to let me die in peace to avoid the suffering. He answered me, all right. He said, "Shut up." God answers every prayer. His answer may be "Yes," "No," "Wait patiently," or "Shut up, I know what I am doing."

Prayer is putting ourselves where God can get to us. It is exposing ourselves to God. It is getting a God's-eye view of our life and the world.

Jesus told a parable about our need to pray always and not to faint or lose heart (Luke 18:1). Either we grow in prayer or we grow faint.

Make your life your prayer and your prayer your life. Prayer is everything you do when you are not saying your prayers as much as when you are praying.

Prayer is the handle of your faith. You must have a handle on your faith to take hold of God's grace.

5

Facing Problems and Making Decisions

All of life is a matter of solving problems by making decisions. Either we resolve our problems or they dissolve us! Either we overcome our problems or they overcome us. Decisive people succeed and win. Indecisive people fail and lose.

To be alive is to have one problem after another. Every problem requires a decision. We must make thousands of decisions every day. Some decision making is automatic and unconscious. Most of our necessary decisions are minor, and we are unaware that we are exercising the decision-making process. The brain readily discerns the situation and sends the proper signals to the muscles and nerves quite automatically.

When there are a number of alternatives, decision making can get bogged down in a quagmire of indecision if we do not learn to make up our minds and do something. When one cannot make up his or her mind, precious time, energy, and life itself are wasted in useless frustration. Knowing what decision to make becomes serious business. A wrong decision can result in serious consequences. Some people are so fearful of making a wrong decision that they make no decision at all.

Some folks have difficulty making up their minds about everything. They are like youngsters in an ice-cream store, looking at all the sweets, flavors, and toppings. Many persons agonize. "What if I make a mistake?" They put off making a decision, they don't sleep, they get nervous, and their whole life becomes one frustration because of their indecisiveness. Is anything more frustrating to oneself and to one's associates than being indecisive about a problem? The good decision maker gets ahead in his or her vocation. The "can't quite decide" person gets nowhere. Indecisiveness keeps a person on edge and results in chronic stress. Some folks have a hard time deciding what clothes to wear for the day or what to eat for breakfast. Worst of all, some folks can't decide what to believe—what is right and what is wrong. In fact, some people can't even decide what is important enough to require a decision.

The first step in problem solving and decision making is to get the problem in perspective. Most of the problems that stagger our minds are not as monstrous as the indecisive mind perceives them to be. The longer we postpone getting those problems into true perspective, the bigger they appear. We put off making our decisions until our entire thinking process becomes confused and distorted. We become so afraid of making a mistake that we do nothing, and the problem swamps us.

When we have what seems to be an impossible problem, we need to open up that problem to God. God has been successful in making infinitely wise decisions and solving world-sized problems since the beginning of time. We must expose our problems to God, for whom nothing is impossible. When we let ourselves see our problems in the light of God's infinite wisdom and trust him to guide us, we will get a God's-eye view of the problem. That will cure us of being so afraid to make a decision. Isaiah wrote (12:2), "Surely God is my salvation; I will trust, and will not be afraid, for the Lord God is my strength and my might." The psalmist, as God's spokesperson, bids us, "Commit your way to the Lord; trust in him, and he will act" (Ps. 37:5). This sounds terribly simple, but that is because we tend to make our problems too complicated. We even make our religion so complicated that we have a hard time believing when a big problem is looming over our heads.

My good neighbor, the Reverend David Gray of the Pleasant Green Baptist Church, captivates me. He came to me one time, asking me to join him in launching a united prayer movement. I did not go along with that program, because for too long I had observed that well-meaning Christians substitute piety for practice. But as I have come to know this man, I see someone who prays all the time—and is always up and doing what he prays! His whole life is his prayer. He prays about everything. He takes God into consideration whether he is brushing his teeth or playing with his little boy. He has had some mighty big problems, ranging from a major health problem to a small power-grabbing group of church members that almost destroyed the congregation when he was convalescing. By praying without ceasing, he always seems to see the worst problems as God sees them—in manageable proportions. He trusts God to help him use his own head and make up his mind to make the right decisions. He is a powerhouse of faith and a powerful force for good in his community.

We must realize that no problems come to us that are not common to most everyone. But with God's help, we have plenty of internal stuff to cope and enough wisdom to decide wisely. Our reaction to any problem, as much as the problem itself, will determine the outcome.

When you have a problem, don't procrastinate in getting at it. While the Bible bids us to "wait patiently upon the Lord," patience is no virtue if you sit around waiting for the problem to solve itself or waiting for God to solve it for you. If your problem is unemployment, don't sit around waiting for the phone to ring or a letter to arrive offering you a choice job. Problems only tend to grow worse with the passing of unused time.

Facing Problems and Making Decisions

When the Bible bids us to wait patiently upon the Lord, it does not mean we are to say our prayers and expect God to make everything happen while we sit idly by, affording the problem more opportunity to grow. Don't wait for God or somebody else to help you. Get busy and help yourself, assured that God will give you the ways and means. Whatever you do, don't expect God to do it all for you. God requires that we use our heads as well as our faith.

Without taking God into consideration, we may convince ourselves that we do not know which way to turn or what to do next when confronted with a difficult problem. As for me, I find great promise in the New Testament letter of James: "If any of you is lacking in wisdom, ask God, who gives to all generously . . . and it will be given you. But ask in faith, never doubting, for the one who doubts is like a wave of the sea, driven and tossed by the wind" (James 1:5–6).

Can you not remember trying to deal with some problem of your own, without God, and feeling tossed about from one possible decision to another, like a wave driven by the wind at sea?

Of course, no decision ought to be made without considering what is God's will and way. Hopefully, we acquaint ourselves with God's word so that, rather than struggling to make up our own mind, we relax and decide things God's way.

Recently I was with a family confronted with the

painful decision either to keep their wife and mother on a mechanical life-support system or to let God's nature take its course. The family prayed to discern God's will and made the decision to let God have his way. This was not a husband or a son playing God. It was a family making a responsible decision that would allow God to work everything together for good with those he loves.

Often there are problems that arise in our lives that we cannot begin to understand. A newborn baby has multiple impairments; a little child suffers from leukemia; a good and beautiful person suffers a damaging stroke. Try to figure it out for yourself and you may lose your mental balance, it is so unreasonable. There are some things we simply must accept and turn over to God—and then trust God to work them out for good in his own time and way. The decision to trust God may be the only possible solution to certain problems. We must trust God and hang on by the thin thread of faith.

The Dutch have an old legend about a spider. This respectable, well-behaved creature lived high up under the rafters of a barn. One day, looking down into the barn, he said to himself, "I wonder what things are like down there?" Being adventurous, he dropped to the end of his long, slender, strong thread until he came to rest on a beam many feet below. Being pleased with the looks of his new surroundings, he wove a web and set up his new house. There he lived as long days went by, catching flies and growing fat and prosperous. Then, one day he noticed the long, slender, strong thread running up into the darkness high above. The spider was puzzled and said, "I wonder what that is for? It serves no purpose that I can see. I can do without it." So he broke the thread—and his little home and world collapsed.

Break that long, slender, strong thread of faith and trust that holds your life securely to God, and your little world can collapse.

Abraham Lincoln told how often, faced with life-and-death problems without ready answers, he was driven to his knees in prayer, because he had nowhere else to turn. He would kneel down weak and rise up with renewed strength. He would bow his head, confused, and come up with a new sense of direction.

Christians turn to God's word not for quick, easy, ready-made answers to difficult problems but to try and understand God's purposes. Between God's word and God's Spirit within us, we have the basic resources to make the right decision.

Sometimes, instead of setting about with God to solve them, we blame our problems on others. We prize our relationship with John Wooden, of basketball coaching fame with UCLA. He is a wise and kindly Christian gentleman. One time at a gathering of young athletes, I heard him say, "Nobody is defeated until he starts blaming somebody else." Too often we settle on fixing the blame rather than fixing the problem.

One of the most serious problems people can have,

without recognizing it, is being indecisive about their own belief system—their religious persuasion. Many people have been hearing about Jesus Christ for years and are well disposed toward him, and that's about it. They never make a personal decision about him.

When the disciples had been with Jesus for some months, he asked them what people thought he was. They responded, "Some say John the Baptist, but others Elijah, and still others Jeremiah or one of the prophets." Then Jesus put a decisive question directly to them: "Who do you say that I am?" He wanted the disciples to make up their own minds about him. Jesus puts that same question to each of us, and he expects a personal decision. Peter made his decision on the spot: "You are the Christ, the Son of the living God" (see Matt. 16:13-17).

I fear that many who are involved in the life of the Christian community, the church, have never made a decision for themselves as to just who Jesus is to them. Their lives are restless with an undiagnosed dis-ease. They wonder what is missing and what is not quite right with their lives. They begin at no beginning and head to no end, simply because they are indecisive. Remember the words of the scripture: "If you confess with your lips that Jesus is Lord and believe in your heart that God raised him from the dead, you will be saved" (Rom. 10:9). Without a definite decision, life may be one unsolved problem, one headache after another. The innate drive to believe, ignored or postponed, only makes the restlessness of life worse. Augustine, who put off making his decision about Christ for years, understood what it means when, according to his *Confessions*, after finally making up his mind, he prayed, "Thou hast made us for thyself, and the heart is restless until it finds its rest in thee."

Whatever the problem, a personal decision is required. Commit yourself to God at the same time that you commit your problem to God. You will not always be absolutely sure you are making the right decision, but having sought God's divine wisdom, take a bold and daring leap of faith and do the best you know to do. That is how God guides us. Faith is always risky. If it weren't risky, it wouldn't be faith. All human experience confirms this: Indecisive persons lose and fail, while decisive persons win and succeed.

6

How to Keep Going When Everything Seems Impossible

Life can be really tough to endure at times. Not even the most pious religious person is immune to trouble. Few persons escape those times when going on seems impossible. When we are up against it in life, heaven may seem so good that we don't want to keep our feet on the ground. So many people live out their lives for years in quiet desperation. Many who keep up a good appearance on the outside are all torn up on the inside.

Let's face it: We are all going to experience times in our lives when things seem impossible to resolve, understand, or even survive. If you have escaped such times so far, look out! You are not likely to escape them indefinitely. No life is always on an even keel. We are all vulnerable to grief, loneliness, sickness, and heartache.

Troubles usually come suddenly, when we are not expecting them. Knowing that these seemingly impossible times are likely to come, it behooves us to be forearmed. Remember: Battles are always won the day before. Those who are prepared survive and thrive. Today is the time to prepare for tomorrow's fights. If our faith is tuned to its full power, troubles will prompt us to claim it and put it to work. Also remember that when things seem impossible, it is only an illusion.

A fellow was telling his pastor about all the things that had been going wrong for him over the past few months. His marriage was falling apart, he had serious conflicts with his son, his mother had died, and he lost his job. He said to his pastor, "I'll tell you, it's enough to make a man lose his religion." The minister said, "It seems to me, Jack, that it's enough to make a man *use* his religion."

We tend to resent reading in the scriptures, "When all kinds of trials and temptations crowd into your lives. . . don't resent them as intruders, but welcome them as friends! Realise that they come to test your faith and to produce in you the quality of endurance [and] mature character" (James 1:2–4, PHILLIPS). We would never develop a saving faith or a mature character were it not for our trials and troubles. When has your faith ever grown without being tested? Who among us would ever grow up without trials? Trouble seems to be the tool by which God shapes us up for better things.

Troubles seem to pile up when we are already worn thin by struggles that seem to have no sign of relief. We reach the point where we don't know what more to do. Either we think it is useless to pray or we don't know what to pray. We either have no feeling of God's presence or we don't care. We get to the place where our mind chases itself in circles, and we can't think straight. Our emotions take over and control us. We feel all tied up in knots. Wild ideas come to us about how to escape it all. We feel we are at the end of our rope and our hope.

The first thing to do in times of trouble is to do something. We have heard that simple statement, "Let go and let God." That may leave us with a bit of faith but no self-initiative. We have no right to expect God to do anything for us when we do nothing more than pray. The fellow who has been terminated by his company after twenty years of faithful and productive service and sits brooding, head in hands and praying, is going to go hungry. The grieving widow who gives up all the things she and her husband enjoyed together, quits going to all the places they used to go, and wallows in self-pity—expecting God to heal her grief and do everything for her—is going to go on weeping and wailing.

When worse comes to worst, don't just turn everything over to God. Do something yourself! God will only help those who first help themselves.

Just what do you do? The apostle Paul advised people to let Christ do, what he wants to do in them. We are to act on whatever faith we have, no matter how little. We are to be aggressive about loving others, instead of expecting everyone to nurse our tender feelings. We are to work our patience. We are to fight the worthwhile battle of faith and keep a firm grip on life (see 1 Tim. 6:11–12).

There are lots of troubles you cannot cure by the Bible, hymnbook, or prayer book, but which you can cure by good personal perspiration and by breathing in some fresh air. I can't help but believe that, were it not for the times and things that seem impossible, our religion would soon rust out.

What turns us to God and renews our sluggish faith more than our trials and troubles? Nothing draws me back to my saving hope in God like those situations that seem impossible to me. It is usually only in times of distress that I even think of the words of the psalmist, "God is our refuge and strength, a very present help in trouble. . . .The Lord of hosts is with us" (Ps. 46:1, 11). Jesus counseled his disciples when they were distressed, "Do not let your hearts be troubled. Believe in God, believe also in me" (John 14:1).

The vine clings to the oak during the fiercest storm, as evidenced in tornadoes. Although the violence of nature may uproot the oak, twining tendrils still cling to it. If the vine is on the side of the tree opposite the wind, the great oak is its protection; if the vine is on the exposed side, the storm only presses it closer to the trunk.

Kansas City's late syndicated columnist Bill Vaughn once wrote, "Stormy weather is what men and women need to remind us that we are not really in charge of any-thing." God is our only ultimate refuge and strength. When we do our part and trust God to do what we cannot do, all things are possible.

When life seems to have fallen in on us, and our little world comes apart, we dare not let ourselves freeze up and become dormant. We must make ourselves do what we know God is expecting us to do. We must not bury our heads in the sand and expect the trouble to go away on its own. We must not deny our trouble, ignore our trouble, or try to escape our trouble. The Bible tells us that we must fight the good fight of faith and hold the course. What is it to fight the good fight of faith? It is holding on, against all odds, to God's guaranteed promise: "My grace is sufficient for you," through thick and thin—through the impossible (see 2 Cor. 12:9).

You may lose a loved one. Suddenly life seems terribly empty. You may not feel like eating. You may wake up in the middle of the night, unable to go back to sleep. You may have no motivation to look after your common re-sponsibilities—or even take care of yourself. In spite of having no incentive, you must keep doing what you know you should do. Also, you must override the pseudo guilt feeling you may experience when you do enjoy something. It is healthy to enjoy good things when going through grief.

Even in the best of households, stress can become so great that things seem impossible to bear. The children get on the tired mother's nerves, or one of the children requires an unusual amount of attention, creating sibling rivalry that borders on violence. If there is a father in the household, he may not be around much of the time. The mother may want to give up, but she keeps herself doing what she knows she must do—and God makes possible what seemed impossible.

Ongoing troubles can threaten the best of marriages. One spouse's idiosyncrasies can try the other's patience. Poor health on the part of one spouse can become very trying. The pressures of employment can back up on the household. Aging parents can bring continuous stress to a marriage. In such situations, each spouse must be determined to be to the other what a responsible partner would be. Both may have to practice tough "unromantic" love, which means exercising disciplined patience, looking for ways of handling difficult situations constructively, ceasing to be touchy, and being stubbornly determined that the love once committed must not fail. In disciplining ourselves to do the right things, even at a time when romantic feelings are lacking, the feelings will always come back —and love will succeed. Only right actions restore romantic feelings.

When life crashes down on us with severe troubles, there is a tendency to panic. When we are scared stiff, we can't think straight. Distressed feelings, unmanaged, can cause us to lose our heads. The New Testament advises us,

"Stand firm." We are to keep our feet on the ground and our mind on God.

Just as a great ship, tossed in a storm, continues her course (perhaps at a slower speed), so we must slowly and confidently face life, do our part to keep moving in the right direction (whatever our feelings or sentiments), and always remember that "God is our refuge and strength, a very present help in trouble" (Ps. 46:1).

We have all discovered that when everything seems impossible, we don't usually feel God's presence. The good news of the Gospel is that God's presence with us is never dependent on our feelings. We may be nauseated by the flu and have no feeling of God's presence. We may be deeply concerned about our finances, a troubled son or daughter, or a serious threat to our own health and have no sense whatever of God's presence or care. What kind of a God would only be with us when we have warm religious feelings? One of the most serious problems facing troubled people is thinking that, because they can't seem to pray or feel God's presence, he is not their abiding strength and help in trouble.

The late Dr. George Buttrick, a noted preacher and theologian, liked to tell the story of a man who came to his study, telling how he had been taken for a ride. Two men had driven him and his car to a lonely spot and threatened his life if he would not agree either to leave the city or refuse to testify in a trial of some New York mobsters. Buttrick asked the man what he did. The man said, "While they waited for my answer, I prayed and without hesitation said, 'Whatever you are going to do, do it quick.'" The minister asked, "What happened next?" The man replied, "I don't know, I don't understand it, but after a few minutes they told me to get back in my car and go." Buttrick asked, "How do you account for the fact that when your life was threatened you were true to the best you know?" After a moment, the man replied, "I guess it was because I could not fail Christ." The pastor responded, "That's only half of it—Christ could not fail you."

The inescapable trials of life can make us or break us; it is up to us to choose which it will be. Trouble is probably the best Christian education textbook in the world. The gem cannot be polished and made valuable without friction, nor can a person be perfected without trials. Christians are to be the photographs of Christ, and it is in the darkroom of trouble and affliction that God develops his finest gems of character.

It is said that when God is going to do something wonderful in a person's life, he begins with a difficulty. If he is going to do something *very* wonderful, he begins with an impossibility. Don't frustrate yourself with the unanswerable question *why?* when you encounter seemingly impossible times. Trust in the Lord and don't rely on your own limited understanding. Rather than distress yourself with *why?* ask yourself *how?* "How will God and I manage this so that I come out better and not bitter?"

When overwhelmed by troubled feelings and seemingly impossible times, be sure to take stock of your learned Christian convictions, not your feelings. The show must go on. Your erratic feelings can wipe you out; convictions of God's faithfulness will always save you.

"Blessed is anyone who endures temptation. Such a one has stood the test, and will receive the crown of life that the Lord has promised to those who love him" (James 1:12).

7

Tips for the Pits

*I*s there anything more miserable or wearing than feeling depressed? Depression, so prevalent today, is nothing new; it has always been the world's number-one public health problem. The Bible tells of many women and men who were depressed because they temporarily lost their faith in God—and thus in themselves. Hippocrates was treating depression back in the fourth century, and the Chinese used herbs to cope with depression long before that. In ancient times depression was thought to be demon possession. It was not until the eighteenth century that the medical nature of depression was uncovered.

Not even saints are immune to depression. The psalmist was distressed with this mysterious disease and cried out, "Why are you cast down, O my soul, and why are you disquieted within me?" (Ps. 42:11). Jeremiah was depressed so often he became known as "the weeping prophet." Isaiah got caught up in depression, letting himself believe he was a failure. Jesus knew depression when he saw all the social evils in the big city, and when his best friends let him down. The apostle Paul became depressed over his own physical pain and all the petty bickering that went on in the church. The encouraging word is that all these people actually grew in faith through these experiences and have left us some practical tips for when we find ourselves in the pits.

Depression plays no favorites among us. Neither is it a respecter of age. Young and old, poor and affluent, educated and uneducated, stable and unstable, sinner and saint—all may plummet to the black hole of depression.

Probably all depression begins with the blues. The blues come and go like the common cold. We don't know when or from where they come. But when the blues hang on and can't be shaken and interfere with normal living, they drag us into depression.

The signs of depression are familiar to most people. We drag around all day, wondering how we will get through it. If the depression is bad enough, we can't get going at all. The person suffering depression bogs down at the least little obstacle, thinks negatively about everything, and sees only emptiness, an impossible future, hopelessness. There seems to be no way out, no options. Inside, the person cries out like Job, Why was I ever born? The depressed person may become so fatigued that he or she becomes emotionless.

Depression affects the soul. The depressed person feels no motivation to pray and tends to withdraw from God and people. Depression is the depressing of all the normal functions—paralyzing one's personality.

We dare not ignore our depression or be insensitive to depression in those around us. Unattended depression can become critical in any of us. Consider a few of the common symptoms:

- Poor self-image or a lack of self-esteem: "I hate me, I'm not OK."
- A feeling of utter hopelessness: "Things will never get any better."
- A sense of failure: "I'm a born loser."
- A load of guilt about all kind of things: "I don't deserve anything good."
- Blaming oneself for everything bad that happens: "It's all my fault."
- Inability to think clearly and make decisions.
- Physical and emotional fatigue, a whipped feeling.
- Lack of motivation and enthusiasm.
- Neglect of one's appearance and grooming.
- A difficult time laughing.
- Spiritual listlessness.
- A lack of interest in sexuality.

We are forever being advised to get in touch with our real feelings. If we deny or ignore our feelings, we get out of touch with reality. We need to get in touch with our feelings and acknowledge them honestly so we are not being ruled by them without knowing it. Usually when we are in touch with our feelings, we can manage them. When we are not in touch with our feelings, they manage us unawares.

A group of psychiatrists headed up by Dr. David Burns at the University of Pennsylvania has become convinced that we feel the way we think. Our emotions result from the way we look at things. It is a neurological fact that before we experience any event we must process it in our mind and give it our own meaning. If our understanding of what is happening is accurate, our emotions will be normal. If our perception is distorted, our emotional response will be abnormal.

The researchers in this human science claim all our moods are created by our thoughts or the way we look at things. We feel the way we feel at any given time because of the thoughts we are thinking. The researchers claim that when we are feeling depressed, our thoughts are dominated by negativity and gloom. We believe things are as bad as we imagine them to be. Every thought becomes pessimistic about the future. These negative feelings causing our emotional disturbance almost always contain gross distortions. Depression is not an authentic experience but a phony counterfeit. We must pinpoint and eliminate the mental distortions that cause us to feel upset.

Dr. Burns likens our blue moods to scratch music coming from a radio that is not properly tuned to the right station. The problem isn't defective transistors or a distorted signal caused by bad weather. We only have to adjust the dials. When we learn to achieve this mental tuning, the music will come through clearly again and our depression will lift.

Illogical pessimistic attitudes make for depression. We feel the way we think. We need to check our thinking to see if it is actual and factual or illusion and fantasy. Think back on the last time you felt depressed. Chances are you had a fantastic ability to believe things that had no basis in reality.

Consider some common distortions in thinking:

• If we fail at some particular thing we tend to think, "I'm a failure at everything." It's a feeling of all or nothing. "If my nose isn't perfect my whole face is ugly." If we have experienced some gross sin, there may well be the feeling, "I'm hopelessly evil through and through, and there can be no salvation for me."

• We tend to overgeneralize. Because something happens once or twice we may tend to assume it is going to repeat itself unceasingly. The student doesn't do well on a test and may get to thinking, "I'm never going to get my degree." A salesman who is turned down on a potential sale may get to believing he will never make it in sales and go off to a bar for the rest of the afternoon.

• We may focus on some negative detail of a given situation and fix our mind on it until we see the whole situation negatively. The subconscious mind running the show is negative, so we see nothing positively. We may focus on a certain undesirable characteristic in our marriage partner until we find fault with everything about that person.

• We tend to eliminate the positive. We need recognition and strokes, but when someone pays us a compliment we turn it down—"Oh, anybody could do that" or "It's a little old thing I got at a garage sale."

• We tend to do a lot of mind reading. We think someone is looking down his nose at us but we never stop to check out the real facts. We hear third-hand that someone said something negative about us and get to thinking everyone hates us without ever checking what the truth may be.

• We tend to make things bigger than they are or reduce them, making them smaller than they are. We exaggerate our faults and minimize our faith.

• We tend to run our life by the seat of our pants, going by our feelings. We accept what we feel as fact. "I feel worthless; therefore, I must be good-for-nothing." "I don't feel like doing anything; therefore, I might as well go to bed." Because something feels negative we assume it is, and we never check out the validity of our feelings.

• We set unreasonable goals for ourselves from old parent tapes: "Be perfect." When the reality of our effort falls short, we feel shame and self-loathing.

• We tend to assume personal responsibility for things and over persons when we have no control. The teacher calls a mother, reporting that her third grader caused a disturbance at the drinking fountain. The mother concludes, "I must be a bad mother. Here is the evidence that I have failed." We confuse influence with control. We cannot assume responsibility for anybody in this world except ourself.

The point of all this is that we tend to believe whatever our depressed brain tells us, and we accept it as absolute truth because it feels real.

This is not an attempt to play the role of a psychiatrist, giving you psychotherapy for the price of this book! However, some tried and proven helps do come out of scripture. You would do well to tuck away these tips for the pits if you would get more life out of living.

We feel the way we think. The way we allow ourselves to think about any situation is the way we feel. An Old Testament proverb states that as a person thinks in the heart, so is that person (Prov. 23:7). Check your thinking. Is it rational and factual in a particular situation?

Don't go by your feelings but do go by your convictions and facts. Your feelings are up and down irrationally, not at all steady and dependable. No matter how you are feeling, do what your intelligent mind tells you to do. Only right thinking can bring about right actions, and only right actions restore right feelings. A stage director of a group of entertainers, who were to make people laugh night after night regardless of their own problems and feelings, voiced a great biblical truth when he is reported to have counseled his troupe before each performance, "Take stock of your convictions, not your feelings. No matter how you feel, the show must go on."

When depressed, get in touch with your learned and experienced convictions. Be sure to go by those convictions, lest your feelings wash you down the drain. Hopefully, you will have developed some sound convictions such as these to run on:

- God is the strength of my life, always my very present help.
- God works in everything for good with those who love him.
- I can do all things through God who strengthens me.
- We may be knocked down but we are never knocked out. We walk by faith, not by sight.

Positive belief always destroys depressed doubts.

We cannot keep any feelings from coming to us, but we can determine how we will manage them. If it is a bad feeling, we don't want to offer it a lounge chair to stay! If we feel hate toward some person, we don't want to go by that emotion but rather get ourselves doing what responsible love would do. If we feel vengeful, let us not take vengeance on ourselves but make ourselves act as a Christian would act. When we feel morbid, let us not act out that feeling but get to doing what a cheerful person would do. Good cheer doesn't always come naturally. We may have to take religiously the psalmist's antidepressant: "This is the day that the Lord has made; let us rejoice and be glad in it" (Ps. 118:24). When we act in good cheer, our feelings follow our actions.

We must help ourselves out of the pits. We are never helpless; we may only allow ourselves to feel helpless. Until we help ourselves with the resources God has given us, God can't help us. We always have options. We must find them. We must keep in touch with reality.

Depression is a very serious business and can be a life-and-death matter. The chronically depressed person may best be served by a well-trained and competent therapist. Don't procrastinate in seeking outside help. God works his healing through good counselors. Very often therapy is needed to clear the way for our faith to be effective.

No mood needs to be our master. God is our Lord and

Master, not our mood. We must fix our mind and heart on him. Out of the laboratory of his own life, Isaiah knew this very well. "Those who wait for the Lord shall renew their strength, they shall mount up with wings like eagles, they shall run and not be weary, they shall walk and not faint" (Isa. 40:31).

8

Keep of Good Cheer

One day during a most crucial period of the Civil War, Abraham Lincoln called a meeting of his cabinet and announced that business of utmost importance would be considered. When the distinguished gentlemen solemnly assembled, the President entered the room and glanced at the circle of anxious faces. He then picked up a book and read one of its most uproarious chapters. Before he had finished reading, the indignation of the cabinet members was painfully apparent. What did the President mean by bringing such men under great pressure to hear a funny story? Mr. Lincoln laid the book down and sighed. "Gentlemen, why don't you laugh? With the fearful strain that is on me night and day, I should die if I did not laugh occasionally. You need this medicine as much as I." Then he took a piece of paper from his hat and read the first draft of the Emancipation Proclamation.

A wisdom writer in the Old Testament wrote, "A cheerful heart is a good medicine, but a downcast spirit dries up the bones" (Prov. 17:22).

If anything should symbolize the Christian faith it is a cheerful heart. The Israelites *celebrated* their God and faith. They developed dances to give their celebration bodily expression. They developed musical instruments to make joyous noises unto the Lord. Their poets wrote of singing trees, laughing trees, and trees that clapped their hands. When we move into the New Testament, there is the celebration of the Messiah in Bethlehem, "Joy to the world." Jesus was the picture of good cheer. His quick wit, sunny smile, and cheerful countenance were contagious so that little children were attracted to him and even rough and tough fishermen. Time and again he bid people, "Be of good cheer." He opened the so-called Sermon on the Mount with the basic formulas of good cheer. He gave his own mission statement: "I came that [you] may have life, and have it abundantly" (John 10:10). He concluded his ministry, saying, "I have said these things to you so that my joy may be in you, and that your joy may be complete" (John 15:11). Paul's letters pick up the same theme: "Rejoice in the Lord always" (Phil. 4:4). The final book of the Bible reveals something of the kingdom of heaven where there is but "fullness of joy for ever more."

This is why I am glad to be a Christian. This is why the Christian faith has such appeal for me. It is no drab, dull dirge. Jesus Christ righting my sinful life with God gives me every reason to be of good cheer, even when my outward circumstances may be less than ideal. Christianity puts a song in the heart and a spring in the step. Some good theologian should develop a doctrine of good cheer. It is a theme written across the pages of the Bible as much as the doctrines of sin and salvation, resurrection and eternal life.

God created us in his own image. The two basic elements he employed were faith and good cheer. A good sense of humor and a cheerful countenance are the natural by-products of being in a right relationship with God. God made us to be happy. A cheerful nature is the normal state of woman and man. A sad countenance is abnormal. A cheerful person is the spiritually healthy person. The sad person is sick.

Two of the Billy Grahams of yesteryear, Theodore Cuyler and Charles Spurgeon, went out into the country for a holiday. They hiked the woods and fields in high spirits. They were heckling each other and laughing, free from care. Cuyler had just told a funny story at which Spurgeon laughed uproariously. Suddenly Spurgeon turned to Cuyler and said, "Ted, let's kneel down and thank God for laughter." Do you ever thank God for healthy laughter? God made us and he knows what is good for us. He knows what he is talking about: "A cheerful heart is a good medicine."

The world seems full of gloomy people. Watch people

in public places, even in church. Gloom writes itself in the wrinkles and lines of their faces. They look as though they carry the problems of the world on their shoulders. These folks tend to think that no one has the right to be cheerful when there are so many troubles and hurting persons everywhere. If these people are right, then Jesus was very wrong. Jesus did everything to make people happy because he knew only happy people seek to solve problems. Unhappy people are too caught up in themselves to have time, care, and concern for others. Only happy people have something to give. Have you ever heard of a sad, pessimistic, whining person contributing anything to the good of others?

We Christians have a new birthright to be happy. We already have our peace with God through our Lord Jesus Christ. The apostle Paul was quick to point out that this does not mean "we have only a hope of future joys—we can be full of joy here and now even in our trials and troubles" (see Rom. 5:1–4, PHILLIPS). Our good cheer isn't reserved in heaven and it isn't dependent on ideal personal circumstances here.

The thing all Christians need today as much as anything we can name is good cheer. It is the Christian faith in the heart that enables us to enjoy the good therapy of wholesome laughter. Oliver Wendell Holmes used to say, "Laughter is God's medicine, and everyone ought to bathe in it." Someone else has said that "laughter is God's soothing touch upon a fevered world." Yet another contends that "humor is one of the finest solvents for the grit of irritation in the gears of life because it helps get rid of conflicts that really do not matter, it disposes of irrelevancies by laughing at them and helps us get a new perspective on naughty problems."

Inevitably when there is a death in a Christian family, deep as the grief may be, laughter will break forth. Often while arranging for the memorial service a family member will recall some funny thing about the deceased, and the grief-stressed family will burst out in spontaneous laughter. The good cheer that a good sense of humor brings with it strengthens the heart and keeps it from breaking. "A merry heart is a good medicine."

If there is anything essential for bearing a Christian witness it is maintaining a good sense of humor. We can be ever so serious about the world's needs and all the hurting people, but if we do not maintain our sense of humor the burden of our concern will destroy us. Dedicated, sensitive, and caring persons without a good sense of humor soon suffer spiritual burnout.

One of our most serious hazards is taking ourselves too seriously. Some Christians seem to think they are responsible for saving the world. We don't save the world or deliver the kingdom, God does.

When we mature in our Christian faith we get to the place where we can laugh at ourselves. One day a little boy by the name of Jimmy Durante was sent off to Sunday school dressed in a Buster Brown suit with knickers and a large flowing bow tie. He stole along self-consciously, hoping none of the guys would see him dressed like this. Then he caught a reflection of himself in a drugstore window and broke out laughing. Some of the guys came along, and one asked, "What are you laughing at, Durante?" Pointing to the reflection in the window, Durante said, "Look, a guy dressed like a sissy with a face like a horse." Soon the others began to laugh, not *at* him but *with* him. The lesson he learned that Sunday was that as long as he could laugh at himself he was safe from the world and safe from feeling sorry for himself.

Phyllis Diller was a homely cleaning woman taking her homeliness seriously. As she grew in faith she learned not to pity herself but she learned to laugh at herself, and the world laughed with her rather than at her. She could say, "Some people are listed in *Who's Who* but I am featured in *What's That?*" She would make audiences laugh, saying, "When my husband tried to run out on me the police arrested him for leaving the scene of an accident."

The single most winsome witness we have to offer our Lord is a cheerful countenance. No sad sack of a Christian ever motivated anyone to taste and see that the Lord is good. A cheerful countenance sets up a chain reaction. An industrial cartoonist was employed to draw a cartoon strip showing the chain reaction of one person's emotions.

The first panel showed the president of the company, in bad humor, reprimanding his superintendent at 8 A.M. The next frame showed the superintendent, angered by management, going out into the shop and taking it out on a workman. The next panel showed the workman arriving home in the late afternoon and taking it out on his wife. The next frame showed the wife spanking the little boy when he came in from play. The final frame showed the boy, made disgruntled by his mother, kicking his pet dog. Some wise guy in the plant penciled in a rough drawing and added it to the strip: The president of the company, walking home past the laborer's house, gets bitten by the dog!

A cheerful attitude is not only a good medicine, it does everyone around you good. If you have Christ in the heart you will have a natural merriment and good cheer to soften the blows of disappointments, lighten daily burdens, brighten any day, endure the worst of stress, and keep you spiritually fit. If you would get more life out of living, practice Jesus' good cheer whether you feel like it or not, and you will think better, study better, work better, relate to others better, feel better, and be better. If by chance you have gotten all wrinkled up with care and personal weariness, it is time for a faith lift!

9

A Sure Cure for Loneliness

*I*s there anything more miserable and degrading than the feeling of loneliness? Scores of people keep the radio or television set on all the time, just to hear human voices. How many people hang around bars in an attempt to escape their loneliness? Some attach themselves to a pet. The widower keeps going back and forth to the cemetery. The high school boy gets to using drugs and dressing differently because of his inner distress. The single adult seeks any kind of relationship, with anyone, out of the desperation of loneliness. The hyperactive youngster, not well accepted by other children, will do most anything to get attention and make someone care one way or another.

By associating with some former members of Kansas City street gangs, we learn that it is loneliness that leads them to join gangs. One young black man claims the gang is the only place he has ever felt accepted.

Alcoholics Anonymous is dedicated to helping persons

who feel so anonymous that they turn to drink; the shy and the timid fill many of the hospital beds on the psych floor.

Most unwanted teenage pregnancies happen between 3 and 6 P.M., when the youngsters are out of school and before they are reunited with the family for dinner. At the root of it is a desperate feeling of loneliness.

What accounts for the majority of the 40,000 suicides in our country every year but chronic loneliness. The symptoms may vary but the sickness is the same: a person's feeling of isolation from God and from neighbors.

Is there anyone who does not feel sick with insufferable loneliness at times? There is the loneliness of night and the loneliness of solitude. There is the loneliness of a crowd. You can be with 70,000 persons at the stadium and feel no relationship with anyone. You are thrown in with everybody and yet you belong to nobody. If you have joy, you can't share it; if you feel blue, you can't express it. Some observers claim that young people appear to enjoy loud blasting music because it is a camouflage for meaningful relationships.

I think of a cheerleader who was most attractive, energetic, and effervescent. She was always surrounded by exciting persons and male admirers, but she was the loneliest little figure in the crowd. There is a local much-cheered athlete and hero to youngsters who, inside, admits to being a desperately lonely man. There is a gentleman most highly respected in the corporate and social community who suffers constantly from the bitter pangs of loneliness. It can be terribly lonely at the top.

Loneliness is the chronic disease of our era. It sickens, warps, incapacitates, and destroys more persons than we ever know. It is a silent killer.

There is an awful danger to loneliness that is not acknowledged and managed. When we are lonely we are weak. Have you noticed that temptations come when we are lonely? It was when Jesus had been out in the wilderness for forty days that he became severely tempted in a number of ways. The tempter seems to know our weakest spot and moment. Ask the person who travels. Ask the person who feels rejected by his or her spouse. Ask the youth with a low self-esteem who doesn't feel accepted by peers at school. When we are feeling lonely we are psychic hermits, subject to every kind of a temptation in the book.

To find a cure for loneliness, we need to get beyond the painful symptoms to find the causes. Anthropologists and psychologists agree that Darwin's hypothesis of the survival of the fittest is a factor of evolution that has played a decisive role in the development of our modern attitudes. Darwin pictured nature as a universal struggle in which human beings and other animals fought to preserve themselves. Life was portrayed always as competition, never cooperation.

However, if we take a closer look at nature we find that it is characterized not so much by competition as by cooperation. Think of the balance in the genius of God's creation. There is the balance of bugs and birds. One kind of life is interdependent with other kinds, like bees and flowers, birds that clean crocodiles' teeth, cattle and grass. Consider the organs of our body. Each is dependent upon others in cooperative unity. All nature bespeaks community and solidarity, not isolation and competition.

Because of our spirit of competition, we tend to use others in the race for personal success. Sometimes when a young man says to a young woman, "I love you," what he means is "I love me; therefore, I want you." Always struggling to preserve ourselves, we tend to fear people because everyone is perceived to be a threat to our place and status. This may cause us to insulate and isolate ourselves. Even little children will exclude others by possessiveness: "What is mine is mine and what is yours is yours only if I can't get it."

We tend to seek happiness as though it were something to be personally and individually owned, whereas it can only be had when shared. No one can enjoy happiness by herself or himself. No one enjoys love alone. No one enjoys laughter alone.

There are husbands and wives who have lived together for years, ever lonely in each other's presence. The wife fears her husband's criticism so she hides some new shoes she has bought for herself until an appropriate time to spring them on him. The husband is afraid to bring up some controversial issue and seeks refuge in an isolated, pouting silence. With no intimate communication about important matters, they just coexist together; secretly lonely, under the same roof. Many people are sick with loneliness in their own homes.

Secrets that couples keep from each other isolate them from each other, resulting in loneliness. It may be a deep remorse for some wrongdoing, certain doubts, jealousies, or resentments. One may have childish daydreams of glory—"What might my life have been like had I married that other person?"—by which the lonely person is consoled. We may conceal such secrets and put on a pretentious front, but secrets make us stand aloof and impersonal. Secrets build walls, when it is bridges that are needed. Love can't stand secrets.

Divorce is resulting in an ever-increasing number of single adults. A single person who resents his or her celibate state is isolated from both self and others. This may cause someone to use another rather than relate to another. Such a person may withdraw and become totally preoccupied with self. Such a person can become a casket person, room for himself or herself but for nobody else.

The Industrial Revolution with its mechanics and machinery contributed to isolating people from one another. Now the information age, with its computers and cottage industries, is once again separating persons, and the epidemic of loneliness worsens.

The mobility of the U.S. population with people moving to a different community every few years, breeds a peculiar loneliness. The population explosion and the crowding of people into impersonal urban centers also contribute to loneliness. Such people think, "Who cares?"

There are things about our social system that contribute to the malady of loneliness. In many schools, children are graded on the curve. This means a better student's grades depend on some students being less competent. Does the youngster on the bottom of the pile feel motivated to cooperate with others or to rebel, drop out, or shut off relationships? Today's lonely youth is saying, "Don't measure and judge me by others, but accept me on my own."

Loneliness is often no more and no less than the fear of being alone. Some people cannot bear the thought of being alone.

Sickness tends to separate us from normal people, and loneliness sets in to worsen our condition.

Loneliness respects no age, race, nationality, economics, or religion. It is every bit as prevalent among the young as among the old. It is found among the rich as much as among the poor. It is found almost as much among the married as it is found among single folks.

Loneliness is a powerful emotion. It can be powerfully constructive or powerfully destructive. Either we take this emotion in hand and do something with it or it will take us in hand and do us damage.

When we go back to the original creation stories in Genesis, we discover that God created us to live in fellowship with him and with our neighbors. We were designed and created to live in community, not solitary confinement. As the one creation story notes, God saw that it was not good for man to be alone (Gen. 2:18).

We must realize that being alone does not mean that one is lonely. Loneliness is a matter of *feeling* alone. The youngster who doesn't get picked to be on the team may feel terribly alone. The person who doesn't get an invitation to the party may feel painfully alone. The man who sees others around him get promotions while he stays in the same position may feel hopelessly alone. The widow suffering the loss of her husband may feel desperately alone. The freshman away at college may get to feeling homesick, awfully alone.

One of the most troubling times in Jesus' life was when all his followers left him and he wondered if his disciples would leave him also. Jesus said, "The hour is coming, indeed it has come, when you will be scattered, each one to his home, and you will leave me alone. Yet I am not alone because the Father is with me" (John 16:32). Not one of us is ever left all alone; God is always with us. Being alone is no reason for feeling lonely.

Feeling cut off from others is of our own making. So many people crave friends but make no effort to be friendly. We can become so concerned about whether we are loved or not that we forget to love. We can become so worked up about not being understood that we don't try to understand. We shut ourselves up crying in self-pity; we forget we must love to be loved.

When we allow ourselves to become separated from God, with whom we have been created to live intimately, we suffer self-inflicted loneliness. When guilty Adam and Eve disobeyed God and tried to hide from him, God was with them as always. When members get angry at the church or the minister and absent themselves, those persons may suffer a painful, unacknowledged loneliness. God is still with these persons, but in their self-inflicted loneliness they don't feel God's presence as before.

When we do wrong and feel guilty, we tend to stay away from church because we feel embarrassed in God's presence. Guilt may cause us to cut ourselves off from God because we feel unworthy and unwanted. Jesus said, "Remember, I am with you always, to the end of the age" (Matt. 28:20).

Guilt, causing us to feel separated from God, is a prime cause of loneliness that even the professional therapist may not pick up. The cure is to accept the fact that God is ever standing by to forgive any and every sin confessed and repented of. All one has to do is accept the Christ who reconciles one to God. How can one ever be lonely in God's love and presence?

The surest cure for loneliness is to practice God's presence. The best promise Christ makes to us is "I am with you always." Notice that there is no condition or limitation: "I am with you to the end of the age." He does not say, "I am with you when you are good." He does not say, "I am with you whenever you feel my presence." God is with us whether or not we feel worthy or sense his presence. Consciously practice God's presence, and you cannot continue to feel lonely. Remember God's promise, "Do not be frightened or dismayed, for the Lord your God is with you wherever you go" (Josh. 1:9). God is with you amid the lonely crowd and at the stadium as well as at the altar, in public school as well as in Sunday school. Keeping meaningfully involved with the church family is one of the surest cures for loneliness. Ask any single or widowed member.

Another sure cure for loneliness is loving our neighbor. The scripture bids us, "Beloved, let us love one another, because love is from God; everyone who loves is born of God and knows God. . . . Beloved, since God loved us so much, we also ought to love one another. . . . If we love one another, God lives in us, and his love is perfected in us" (1 John 4:7, 11–12).

There is no greater therapy for loneliness than loving our neighbors. Lots of people around us are lonely too. One has to *be* a friend to *have* friends. The old saying holds true: "Seldom can a heart be lonely if it seeks a lonelier still."

A youngster came home from camp, her first time away from home. Asked if she was homesick, she replied,

"I didn't have time. I was so busy trying to keep other girls from being homesick, I didn't think about being lonely myself."

We may assist God in curing our loneliness by seeking out others who are lonely. Individuals who have gone through a particular experience are the very ones to understand and help others in the same situation. The widow can best help another widow. The divorcée can best help another divorcée. Involving oneself in seeking the betterment of others draws one away from self-pity and self-centeredness. Loneliness and self-centeredness are first cousins.

Praying for others is another cure for loneliness. Praying for others relates one's life to others. Praying for others has been called "the most ancient friendship of all believers." When you are praying for others you are relating your life to them. For those who are lonely, prayer is the means by which a person can be brought back to life.

Be cheerful whether you feel like it or not. People tend to be as cheerful as the people around them. Cheerfulness is contagious and has a chain reaction upon those around us. A sour countenance will drive others away, making for more loneliness.

The next time you feel lonely, get the lead out of your spirit. Instead of sitting around thinking about how bad you feel and wallowing in your own miserable self-pity, find another lonely person and get started doing something for that person. Love another person, and you will feel the presence of God as your own companion. Jesus gave us the secret of life when he said that it is in losing our life for his sake and the sake of others that we find it (see Matt. 16:25).

But be forewarned. You must be willing to pay the price of loneliness to stand by your convictions. The higher your character the more you may repel some people, as well as attract others. The person willing to pay the price of loneliness to stand by God and good, no matter where everyone else is, will never walk alone. One man has said, "I am left alone as my Master was; I am hated by some who loved me once, not for what I do but for what I think." Remember, you never walk alone; being with God makes for company. And if we love one another, God lives in us.

10

Practice Patience

Many times I have prayed impulsively, "Lord, give me patience—a double portion, quickly!" Who of us does not want instant patience several times a day?

Like most Americans, I was raised to hurry. How many times I heard at home, "Hurry up, Bobby!" Many times teachers would say to me, "Quit dawdling!" From my earliest days, I learned not to wait for anything. Today, we want fast food service. We want pollsters and computers to give us election results before people even finish voting. I find myself champing at the bit when using an older word processor printer that takes three minutes to print one page. One of the most popular $125 seminars on the market is on time management.

My emotions get all out of sorts when I am in the grocery store and the person ahead of me doesn't even start to make out his check until after the total is called out. It is equally disquieting to approach the drive-in window of the bank, only to have the character in the car ahead chat with the teller before even starting to make out his deposit slip. These experiences tax my nerves as much as seeing the radar patrol car on a side street just as I am crowding the accelerator a bit—having been delayed at the store and the bank and now being late for my appointment. Can you identify with these causes of impatience?

Impatience saps our strength, tightens our stomach, tenses our muscles, and racks our nerves. Impatience results in bad judgment, impulsive behavior, accidents, crimes, child abuse, and spouse bashing (emotional or physical). Impatience gives rise to all kinds of hostility—even wars.

A man who had just made a serious mistake exclaimed, "If only I had been patient a bit longer, I would not have blown the whole thing!"

A young mother was overheard to say, "When I am tired and irritable, I don't have a bit of patience with the children. It isn't fair that they must take the brunt of my impatience."

Charlie Brown, on one of his visits to the five-cent psychiatrist, wanted to know why he didn't have patience. Lucy counseled him with some age-old wisdom, "Patience is genius. Can't you see your problem, Charlie Brown?"

Life has its built-in waiting stages that require patience. The small child must wait until he or she is old enough to ride a two-wheeled bicycle. The teenager must wait until age sixteen to drive a car. The medical student must wait for a diploma. The young couple must wait until they have saved enough of a down payment to qualify for buying a house.

You have heard of the naturalist who was studying a cocoon. Inside, a butterfly was struggling to get out. The scientist heard it beating against the sides of its little prison, and his heart went out in pity to the helpless thing. He cut away a section of the cocoon and released the little captive, but it wasn't the beautiful creature he expected. It lay helplessly on the table. It could not even walk, let alone fly. Instead of beautifully colored wings, they were weak, shriveled, colorless stubs. What was the matter? The cocoon wall had been removed too soon, before the struggler had developed sufficiently through struggling to be ready for a glorious flight among the flowers and into the sunny skies.

Listen, anxious parent! There is divine purpose in your struggles and problems with your children—those things that breed impatience in you. You would never become a wonderful parent, nor would your children become lovely children, were it not for the struggles and trials that try your patience.

In his New Testament letter, James wrote, "Whenever you face trials of any kind, consider it nothing but joy, because you know that the testing of your faith produces endurance; and let endurance have its full effect, so that you may be mature and complete, lacking in nothing" (James 1:2–4).

The good life requires patience. The farmer must wait

patiently for planting time, rain, sunshine, and the harvest. He cannot speed up any of these. If he does not wait patiently, there will be no harvest. We read in the Old Testament, "There is . . . a time to be born, and a time to die; a time to plant and a time to pluck up what is planted; . . . a time to weep, and a time to laugh; a time to mourn and a time to dance" (see Eccl. 3:1–8). The writer clinches the passage, "He [God] has made everything suitable for its time" (Eccl. 3:11).

We must adopt the rhythm of nature if we are to claim the fruits of God's providence. God has made a world in which things move at their natural pace.

Patience is second only to love in the Christian graces. When the apostle Paul listed the virtues of love, he listed patience as the first virtue and the last virtue. He noted that love is patient. Then he listed its other virtues: "Love is kind; love is not envious or boastful or arrogant or rude. It does not insist on its own way; it is not irritable or resentful; it does not rejoice in wrongdoing." He concluded his list of love's qualities: "It bears all things, believes all things, hopes all things, endures all things. Love never ends. . . . And now faith, hope, and love abide, these three; and the greatest of these is love" (1 Cor. 13:4–6, 13).

We see the patience of God in Jesus. How patient and forbearing he was! Crowds would hound him until he had no space for himself. Time and again, the disciples let him down, but he never lost hope in them. He would teach them, and they would forget, so he would teach them again. He was mocked and scourged, but he would only pray, "Father, forgive them; for they know not what they do" (Luke 23:34, KJK).

One of the greatest heroes of the Bible is Abraham, who is respected today by Jews, Christians, and Muslims alike. He had to learn patience. He was rich, successful in business, and very religious. He believed that God would keep his word and give him a son. However, he and Sarah became impatient by the time he was eighty-six and Sarah was in her seventies. At Sarah's urging, Abraham impregnate Sarah's Egyptian maid, who subsequently bore a male child. At first, this seemed like a good way to hurry God along. But the birth of Ishmael brought on all kinds of marital problems and conflict between the young maid and the aging Sarah. The result of Abraham's impatience was stress, immorality, and intolerance for the next fourteen years. While Abraham and Sarah were in a hurry, God was not. In God's own time, Isaac was born to them.

Because of our fallen nature, we have a natural bent toward impatience. Time and time again, the Bible bids us to be patient, to show forbearance, to be steadfast, to endure, to wait, and to persevere. Our fallen nature causes us to do just the opposite: to be impatient, impulsive, and angry and to give up because we will not wait.

John Calvin confessed, "I have not so great a struggle with my vices, great and numerous as they are, as I have with impatience. My efforts are not absolutely useless; yet I have never been able to conquer this ferocious wild beast."

John and Charles Wesley, fathers of Methodism, had a very patient mother. Her husband once said to her, "I marvel at your patience! You had told the blockhead the same thing twenty times." Susanna Wesley looked fondly at the child and said, "Had I spoken the matter only nineteen times, I should have lost all my labor."

Patience is the price of success. Edward Gibbon worked twenty years writing *Decline and Fall of the Roman Empire.* Noah Webster labored thirty-six years writing his dictionary. William Cullen Bryant rewrote one of his poetic masterpieces ninety-nine times before publication—and it became a classic. Charles Goodyear spent ten years of study, poverty, and public ridicule developing hard rubber. George Westinghouse was treated as a wild kook by most railroad executives for years. "Stop a train with air?" Only by patient perseverance did he finally sell the idea of the air brake. One of our missionaries stuck it out in Africa for fourteen years before having even one convert. Simply for want of patience, many never hang in there long enough to be successful and receive God's best providence.

If God made us after his own image, he made us to be patient. How many times in the Bible do we read that God is "slow to anger and abounding in steadfast love" (e.g., Ps. 103:8). What if God lost patience with you and me? Who would stand?

Another word in the Bible for patience is translated "endurance." The hallmark of love is patience: Love endures all things; loves stands when it seems like everything else has fallen. This word for patience is used in relation to time. It is waiting until the appointed time has come without becoming irritable. Endurance speaks of the strength of patience. It can endure anything and still stand.

We must remember that patience is sometimes only quiet, confident waiting, when we cannot do anything about a given situation. Our child may be deathly ill in the intensive care unit of the hospital. There may not be a thing we can do except entrust the child to God and wait upon God. Someday we may experience the worst of the aging process and be able to do nothing more than put ourselves in God's care and wait upon him. In his blindness, unable to fulfill his dreams, John Milton wrote, "They also serve who only stand and wait."

One of the New Testament assurances that spurs me on when I become impatient is found in Galatians 6:9, "Let us not grow weary in doing what is right, for we will reap at harvest-time, if we do not give up."

We may think of Job as the model of patience. We often hear the expression "the patience of Job." When we look at Job, we see that patience is anything but passive. Job resented the circumstances that came upon him through no fault of his own. He questioned the conventional and orthodox arguments of his friends. He agonized over the unbearable thought that God had forsaken him. The great fact about Job is that, in spite of his torment, stress, loss, and questions, he never for a moment lost his confidence in God. He could say, "Though he slay me, yet will I trust in him" (Job 13:15, KJV).

The New Testament word for patience is dramatized in Job. He goes through all the crises of doubt, sorrow, and the loss of everything except his life and hangs in there with a faith that becomes stronger by way of its testing. Any faith that endures through unanswerable questions, honest doubting, and emotional torture is going to come through victorious. Who of us has not observed persons who struggle when it looks like God has forsaken them, grit their teeth, clench their fists, and cling to the remnants of their faith until they are able to see that God is good and a very present help in trouble? Because Job hung in there through it all, the scripture notes, "The Lord blessed the latter days of Job more than his beginning" (Job 42:12).

I don't think that patience can be taught. It is caught from God's Spirit within us. The Bible tells us, "The fruit of the Spirit is . . . patience" (Gal. 5:22). So long as we practice God's presence, we practice patience. No one gets much real life out of living except by patience. Patience is the practice of all the Christian virtues at the same time. Patience is concentrated strength afforded us by the grace of God.

11

How We Temper Our Temperament

I have gone back into the laboratory of my own life and my observations of others to try and understand something of human anger. I was brought up in my childhood with the parental message that anger is evil—especially if you vent it openly. I never saw my parents show what I thought was anger. I suspect that my sensitive mother was often hurt, and hurting was the way her anger was internalized.

I never recognized anger in myself. Our firstborn, never having seen anger, did not know how to deal with it. A counselor urged us to stage an angry conflict that the lad could observe. It was a dramatic show for both son and parents, but he did learn from it.

Some years into our marriage, my good wife enabled me to see that getting quiet and withdrawing was my way of expressing anger—in what I thought was a safe, sane, and righteous way. To this day it is difficult for me to recognize anger and express it openly. The times when I have vented it, I have not liked what it did to me or how it caused me to lose my cool. This unhealthy way of dealing with natural anger puts great stress on body and spirit. It may or may not be a significant point, but my mother died at a relatively early age.

• John gets criticized by the boss and feels the criticism is unfair. He says, "I'm chastised again, when I'm not even responsible for what happened." He is mad and no longer enjoys his job.

• Joanne says, "I do everything to please people. I do whatever they want me to do, but they never appreciate it." She is an angry person.

• Jim is on a committee. There is one person on the committee who talks endlessly, and nobody knows just what he is saying. Jim comes home from the meeting so angry he doesn't want to go back.

• A fellow is disciplined, and his wounded ego festers with anger until he does all kinds of irrational things to vindicate himself. His anger becomes chronic and literally takes control of his life.

• A man comes home from a football game when the Chiefs have lost and is furious with the quarterback and the defense team. His wife claims he is hardly himself for the next forty-eight hours.

• A woman is upset because she feels she has blown a job she was working on. "How could I be so dumb?" she asks herself. She is angry with herself.

• A woman's husband betrays and deceives her. She should divorce him but knows she would be left with the children and inadequate financial support. She is angry that she is the one who has to suffer, when he is the unfaithful "bed hopper."

• A mother and father have a very difficult time conceiving a child. They go through all kinds of fertilization programs at great expense. Finally, they have a child, and in only a few months the child dies. The parents are so angry with God that they vow never to set foot in church again.

• A youngster isn't particularly good in sports. He is always the last one to be chosen for a pickup game of soccer. It makes him so mad to always be the last choice that he is a bear when he gets home.

Being created in God's image, we all have a natural capacity for anger, just as we have a natural capacity for love. Our anger is likely to be in proportion to our love. Our capacity to love what is good determines our capacity to hate what is evil. Scripture confronts us with a God whose anger pervades the Hebrew Testament (as I prefer to call the Old Testament), and the Christian Testament reveals Jesus, who often became very angry.

We do not need to be apologetic or ashamed of our anger, because it is a given in our human nature. Our temper can be good or bad, constructive or destructive, righteous or rotten.

There is no way one can ever claim to be a Christian and not be downright angry with the genocide of six million Jews, Muslims starving to death, thousands of women raped, one out of ten children emotionally and physically abused, and handguns easily accessible to kids—I would not be true to my calling if I did not rise up with anger over the injustices (and the unjust) that warp people's souls, disenfranchise hundreds of thousands, and grind so many of the world's people into dust. Who of us would not concur with the New York Supreme Court, which declared, "A society that loses its sense of outrage is doomed to extinction."

Others besides me were raised in homes where we were taught, in one way or another, that feeling anger is evil—and it is even worse to vent it. Some well-meaning parents take scripture out of context, quoting Jesus when he said, "If you are angry with a brother or sister, you will be liable to judgment" (Matt. 5:22). It is dangerous to grow up denying your natural anger. Anger denied does all kinds of injury to the human personality. Good anger denied deprives society of reform.

How We Temper Our Temperament

Feelings of anger, when ignored, denied, or put off, stay with us and often result in hypertension, migraine and other headaches, colitis, certain types of arthritis, depression, and self-hate. People who deny their anger may be given to compulsive drinking, overeating or other eating disorders, insomnia, and silent pouting. When we do not acknowledge our anger, we turn our anger inward and hurt ourselves in many different ways.

We may fool ourselves about our anger, but we cannot fool our arteries, blood pressure, or digestive tract. Many persons who always cover their anger suffer peptic ulcers, colitis, sore necks, skin rashes, or heart disease! When there is discord in the mind, there will be discord in the body.

Traditionally, it was thought that there were only two ways to respond to anger: fight or flight. It was thought that an angry person turns either inward or outward. Turning inward is unhealthy, because you only internalize your aggression and take on resentment like a sponge absorbs water. Some people think that if you turn outward and vent your anger, you will feel better. But just getting your feelings out in the open doesn't necessarily make things right.

The story is told of a woman who took her husband to a psychiatrist for an evaluation. In time, the psychiatrist came out to confer with the wife. He said, "I regret to tell you that your husband has lost his mind." The wife replied, "I'm not surprised. He has been giving me a piece of it every day for forty years!"

It is time we realize that we have more than these two options, fight or flight, turning inward or outward. We can control our anger, temper our temperament. The apostle Paul wrote the Ephesians, "Be angry but do not sin; do not let the sun go down on your anger. . . . Let no evil talk come out of your mouths, but only what is useful for building up, as there is need, so that your words may give grace to those who hear. And do not grieve the Holy Spirit" (Eph. 4:26, 29–30). We do not have to be plagued with excessive irritability that sours the soul and sickens the body, and we can be angry without having to sin.

We could not talk about managing our anger without being reminded of what a wise Greek philosopher and many others have said, "Know thyself." Each of us needs to check our IQ—our irritability quotient. When we are willing to know ourselves—to acknowledge our anger—we can begin to manage our feelings.

Who makes you mad? Because you are angry at someone, you cannot blame that person for making you angry. No one can make you angry unless you give the person that power over you. You are making yourself angry by allowing yourself to think of that person in a way that gives you angry feelings.

Tempers are like runaway horses, unless they are controlled they can take us where we do not want to go. When we lose control of our temper, we are temporarily insane. That is why a normally decent person can become angry enough to shoot another if a gun is readily available. Some people can become so angry it affects their vision. An optometrist claims he can never examine the eyes of an angry person—such a person literally cannot see straight.

When we lose our temper, we lose our head and our ability to think rationally. The question for the normally intelegent person is not whether we should feel angry but what to do with that emotion. Even if we have every reason to be angry, how can this anger be useful? Will it help achieve a desired goal, or will it defeat our purpose?

We saw an example of the wrath of God when the Israelites, his chosen people, forsook him and turned to idols and false gods. God's wrath is always provoked by love. By the constructive use of his divine wrath, he saved his people and they became reconciled. Jesus became very angry when he saw people turn his Father's house of prayer into a house for profit. In touch with this feeling of anger, he was in control of it; his anger moved him to reform the temple. The anger of God is also evidence of his love. His anger always communicates not only his will but also his saving, redemptive love. We read in scripture that whoever God loves, he chastens.

Some Christians think there is no place for anger in a Christian marriage. Because there is love, there is going to be anger at times. Over control your anger and you over control your love. If you are to love normally, you must allow for normal anger. The secret of managing your temper in marriage is making sure you always stick to the *issue* and never pick on the *person*. Where there is true love there will be constructive anger—redemptive anger. The old proverb is true: "The anger of lovers renews the strength of love." I hate to think where I would be today were it not for my wife's saving anger.

The Bible tells us that God is slow to anger but doesn't hold back his wrath too long (see Num. 14:18 and Ps. 103:9). If God repressed his anger he would not be a just, holy, and loving God.

Don't feel sinful when you have angry feelings. You can't help it. Don't suppress them because you are afraid of yourself when you are mad. Don't deny your angry feelings because you think good Christians should never feel anger. Don't procrastinate in dealing with those angry feelings, thinking they will go away. As the apostle Paul counseled (Eph. 4:26), "Do not let the sun go down on your anger." Get at it readily. Chances are you will not be able to manage your angry feelings on your own. Only God's grace is sufficient to manage your temperament. One of the gifts of the Spirit promised the believer is "self-control" (see Gal. 5:22). When we own Christ as Lord of our whole life, he enables us to control our feelings—even raging anger. Without that control, the most wonderful persons can do the most irrational things in a fit of temper.

One could hardly deal with the subject of anger without quoting Aristotle's wise observation: "Anybody can become angry, that is easy; but to be angry with the right person, and to the right degree, at the right time, for the right purpose, and in the right way is not easy."

We must depend on the Spirit of God within us to enable us to mind our anger. When we lose our temper, we lose our head—and our whole control system goes out of whack. There is that proverb, "Those with good sense are slow to anger" (Prov. 19:11). It is God-sense that enables us to use our temper constructively.

It is good to have a good temper. With a good temper, we will protect what is right and resist what is evil. A tempered temper is what makes for healthy righteous indignation, which is also called "character." Peter was a very temperamental person, but once he gave himself to follow Christ, God used his temper as one of his best assets. What God can do with a person's temper once he has a person's heart!

There must be a capacity for anger in the Christian's life, but it must be the right kind of anger. Selfish anger is bad. Anger at what happens to oneself is bad. Crossness, bad temper, and irritability are bad. But unselfish anger is good. Anger over what is happening to cause someone else pain is a good unselfish anger. Without such unselfish anger, the world would go to pot. Thank God for Abraham Lincoln's unselfish wrath when he saw African Americans being auctioned off as slave property. Our country would be another Bosnia today had it not been for the unselfish anger of Martin Luther King, Jr., who managed that anger for good in nonviolent ways.

There were times when Jesus was majestically angry. He was angry when the scribes and the Pharisees were watching to see if he would dare to heal the man with a withered hand on the Sabbath (see Mark 3:5). It was not wounded ego, injured by their criticism, that angered him so. He was angry that their hardened fundamentalist orthodoxy would impose unnecessary suffering on a neighbor.

Anger that is selfish always tends to be passionate and uncontrolled. Selfish anger is evil and must be surrendered to Christ. Anger that is channeled into the service of our Lord and our neighbors is one of the most dynamic forces at our command.

Always use your temper, don't lose it. Your anger can be a powerful force for good. Being fired up with righteous indignation makes you one of God's best servants. Be careful, however, for the angry mind will tend to mistake the selfish anger of the wounded ego for righteous indignation. Surrender your anger to the Lord of your life, and he will make your anger work for you, not against you. Give your temper to God. He can use it!

12

Spiritual Health Care

*Y*ears ago I heard a story about the famed electrical engineer and physicist Charles Steinmetz. Asked what line of research would see the greatest development in the future, he said the greatest development would be in the spiritual area. Here is a force that, as history clearly teaches, has been the greatest power in the development of humankind. We have only been playing with it and have never seriously studied it, as we have the physical forces all around us. Someday people will learn that material things do not bring happiness and are of little use in making men and women creative and powerful. Then the scientists of the world will turn their laboratories over to the study of God and prayer and the spiritual forces that as yet have hardly been investigated.

Many of us live as if we are no more than a physical body—animal life. You see some health freaks who jog early in the morning or late at night with the most forlorn and painful look on their faces. Many people are hypo-chondriacs, supersensitive about every little pain or ailment. Everyone is concerned about physical health care reform. How are we going to afford needed attention for our gallbladder, kidneys, lungs, arteries, bones, eyes, ears, uterus, or prostate? Nothing concerns us more than how we receive care and what it costs to keep our bodies functioning comfortably on the inside and looking handsome on the outside.

Sex therapists are overworked these days when people go on television to tell Oprah Winfrey and her audience how they have gotten help when their bodies were not deriving sufficient pleasure. Notice the fanatical attention we give our body's weight and shape. The media keep us informed about what we put in our bodies, with programs and pieces about bacteria-infected chicken, filth in pack-inghouses, pesticides on fruits and vegetables, blood cholesterol levels, and tooth-decaying carbohydrates. Teenage girls starve themselves half to death to stay in a size 8. Boys will work out and pump iron until they can hardly stand up in order to have the macho body build they see in magazines.

Women and even men spend millions every year to look beautiful or handsome and wear the latest Chanel or Polo scent. We have come to a time in society when we attend the physical body with an idolatrous worship. It is as though we do not think of ourselves as more than flesh, bones, skin, nerves, and muscles.

What we won't do to save a life, and we do so little to save a soul!

The apostle Paul wrote to the Christians in Rome, "Those who live according to the flesh set their minds on the things of the flesh," and "To set the mind on the flesh is death" (Rom. 8:5, 6).

Apparently many people never think of themselves as more than flesh. Rather than understanding sexuality as the physical expression of spiritual love in the covenant relationship of marriage, with many it is no more than a biological relief.

Surely we are more than animal life. God made us but a little lower than himself, so the psalmist tells us (see Ps. 8:4, 5). In the Genesis story God breathed his own breath into a physical form, and woman and man became living human beings. In scriptural language, breath and spirit are of the same word. Breath or spirit is absolutely essential for life. The same word in scripture means wind. Wind always has the idea of power, as in the "rush of a violent wind" on the day of Pentecost (Acts 2:2). For Paul, Spirit represented a divine power. When we have no breath we die. When we do not have the lifegiving Spirit of God we are powerless. It is the Spirit-breath of God breathed into us that makes us unique from all other animal life.

What is it to be spiritual? It is to be related to God, with the relationship the basis for all other human relationships. "You shall love the Lord your God with all your heart, and with all your soul, and with all your mind" and "You shall love your neighbor as yourself" (Matt. 22:37, 39).

When Paul used the word "flesh" he usually meant human nature in all its weakness and its vulnerability to temptation and sin—our sinful nature apart from God. He meant our human nature with the body's drives, instincts, and passions. He meant everything that attaches a person to the world rather than to God. He meant a life dominated by the desires and drives of sinful human life instead of a life dominated by the desires and love of God. When he referred to the sins of the flesh he was not thinking any more about sex than he was about hatred, idolatry, uncontrolled anger, jealousy, drunkenness, and bad attitudes (see Gal. 5:19–20). To the apostle, "flesh" was human nature—all that a person is without Christ.

Before Paul came to accept Christ for himself, he was at the mercy of his own weak human nature, with its fleshly appetites and raw animal instincts. But when he came to receive Christ to himself there came a surging power of the Spirit of God that freed him from the human nature that once dominated him. In Christ his life became dominated by the Spirit of power, the Spirit of God, which dominates us with a power not our own.

There is an old saying, "The spirit is willing but the flesh is weak."

We tend to associate spirituality with serenity or peace of mind. Many persons never know real peace of mind or calmness of nerves. They are not at peace with God, the world, or themselves. Augustine was plagued with restlessness until he found what had been missing in his life—God. Augustine prayed, "Lord, thou madest us for thyself, and we can find no rest till we find rest in thee."

We give most of our life to making a living more than to making a life. Jesus said, "One does not live by bread alone, but by every word that comes from the mouth of God" (Matt. 4:4). One can be fed daily with Wonder Bread and be spiritually starved. There is as much a hunger in the human soul as there is a hunger in the human stomach. Jesus said, "Blessed are those who hunger and thirst for righteousness, for they will be filled" (Matt. 5:6). By neglecting the hunger of the human spirit, many of us suffer a sickly spiritual malnutrition.

Jesus said, "I am the bread of life. Whoever comes to me will never be hungry" (John 6:35). As necessary as daily bread is for the body's health is Christ for the soul's health.

Some Christians practice a more mystical kind of spirituality. "Mystic" is a word some people interpret to mean "otherworldly," an existence apart from ordinary life. These folks give themselves to one kind of meditation or another, eagerly striving to feel at one with the Infinite. They say that religion is what we do with our solitariness. Faith for mystics is an ecstatic state of being grasped by mystery. Some get so caught up in the "otherworld" they scarcely touch base with this one. However, some of these mystics do stress the need for service to the poor and needy. Their ultimate goal is union with God, but works of love are their road to this union. The dominant motif of Christian mysticism is expressed in Augustine's axiom, "Through the man Christ you reach the God Christ."

The more typical spirituality also centers on the divine–human encounter. It is not so much being touched by mystery as being confronted by the living Savior. For us, faith has a rational content. This spirituality centers in God's grace, the favor of God, not a mysterious power infused into someone by which the person becomes divine. This spirituality sees the believer as a repentant sinner, not a divinized being. This spirituality sees obedience to God as our prime concern. The basis of our salvation is in what God has done for us, not in striving and seeking God.

In this spiritualism, prayer is more a wrestling with God, as for Jacob, than a quiet, passive meditation on God.

Both styles of spiritualism call us to walk by faith, not by sight. Both are of the mind of Jesus that nothing is as important as loving God, and both would insist that love for God must overflow in love for one's neighbors. We are called not simply to personal sanctity but to social holiness.

Christian spirituality is both inward and outward. The Christian faith holds both to the historical Christ and the indwelling Christ, the mystical Christ. The French philosopher and theologian Blaise Pascal said, "Happiness is neither without us nor within us. It is in God, both without us and within us."

It is by way of our spiritual nature that we have eternal life. The Bible tells us that when our physical body dies we are given a spiritual body by which our personal life goes on. What is born of the flesh dies; what is born of the spirit lives forever (read 1 Corinthians 15). In view of this, why are we so totally preoccupied with our temporal physical health and unconcerned about our eternal spiritual health?

How do we attend our spiritual health? The very words "spirit" and "spiritual" suggest the work of God's Holy Spirit. In this very book it is not so much the writer and the reader dealing with the Holy Spirit as it is the Holy Spirit dealing with us. The spiritual life depends on the Spirit of God incorporated into our life and the Holy Spirit dwelling in the community. When our spirit and God's Spirit are in touch, we enjoy our best all-around health.

In talking about the Holy Spirit let it be understood clearly that we are talking about the very presence of the resurrected living Christ. Once Paul embraced Christ for himself, he said, "It is no longer I who live, but it is Christ who lives in me. And the life I now live in the flesh I live by faith in the Son of God, who loved me and gave himself for me" (Gal. 2:20).

Paul also said, "Do you not know that you are God's temple and that God's Spirit dwells in you?" (1 Cor. 3:16).

To keep spiritually fit requires certain disciplines, just as keeping physically fit does. These spiritual disciplines are prayer, intelligent Bible study, repentance, obedience, simplicity of lifestyle, public worship come Sunday, and participation in the Lord's Supper.

It is primarily by our public worship in spirit and in truth that God transcends our being. The Spirit of God is first given to the community of believers and then to the individual (read Acts 2). It is by worship that Spirit with spirit doth meet. To keep consciously in touch with God requires praying constantly. Praying is simply practicing God's intimate presence within us. Prayer means listening to God more than talking to God. Believe me, prayer is much more than what some devotional manuals suggest—moments of prayer while the traffic light is red!

To keep spiritually fit we must search and research God's word. God's word claims to be the very power unto our salvation (Rom. 1:16). Be very careful you relate to Bible teachers who really know the Word in its context. There are so many well-meaning and zealous Bible teachers out there who have missed the real meaning of the texts. All parts of scripture are to be interpreted by Jesus' life and teachings. He is God's "last word."

To keep spiritually fit we must center our whole life on Christ. Without Christ, life gets out of balance and is only one headache after another. Christ is our health and salvation.

When we are spiritually fit we have an immune system that wards off temptations, sins, depression, and all the diseases that strike at the mind and the heart. The spiritually fit are most likely to be physically fit because our spirit affects every part of our anatomy.

To keep spiritually fit we must exercise our faith. Physical muscles that are not exercised will atrophy. Faith not exercised dries up. Jesus said, "Not everyone who says to me, 'Lord, Lord,' will enter the kingdom of heaven, but only the one who does the will of my Father in heaven" (Matt. 7:21). Jesus' brother wrote in his New Testament letter, "A man is justified before God by what he does as well as by what he believes. . . . Yes, faith without action is as dead as a body without a soul" (see James 2:24,26, PHILLIPS).

The prophet Micah tells us exactly what God wants of us (6:8): "And what does God require of you but to do justice, and to love kindness, and to walk humbly with your God?"

We can strive to be spiritual, but if we do not do the physical works of God as we go about in our social circles, political arenas, places of business, law practices, corporate management, and family life, our spirituality is a hoax. True Christian spirituality requires us to do what God would have us do even when it may not feel comfortable or be easy or popular or even succeed for a time. If our spirituality does not express itself in our deeds, it is not for real. True spirituality means obedience as much as it means adoration.

God promises, "I will pour out my spirit upon all flesh" (Joel 2:28).

If you would get lots more life out of living every day, don't neglect your spiritual nature. It is as real and as significant as your physical nature.

13

Putting New Life and Romance into Worn Marriages

• These days they are saying an old-fashioned couple is not one that *stays* married but one that *gets* married!

• Many a woman has married a man for life—only to discover he doesn't have any.

• "I made an appointment for us with a marriage counselor," the wife told her husband, "but you don't have to go. I can speak for both of us."

• An older fellow said, "Before we got married my wife used to say, 'You're only interested in one thing.' Now I can't even remember what it was."

• Twin beds became popular when women began to realize they should not take their troubles to bed with them.

• The story of some marriages is all in the scrapbook.

While we may joke about marriage, it is still the most cherished relationship known this side of heaven. Marriage is not going out of style. This is evidenced by the fact that most widowed and divorced persons yearn to marry again. Many divorced persons feel that even a less than an ideal marriage is better than no marriage. While there are single persons mature enough to find creative fulfillment in life, most of us feel we need marriage to be complete.

Divorce always seems to be on the increase in this country. More couples married thirty years or longer are separating. It would not be reasonable to insist that couples stay married under all circumstances. Very often divorce seems to be the lesser of two evils and therefore the moral thing to do. There is no virtue in two persons remaining married and emotionally murdering each other!

The great concern is that for every divorce there are two marriages going on in cold coexistence for the sake of outward respectability. For every dead marriage terminated in court, two more are dying on the vine. More and more young adults are scared to death of marriage, having observed the unions their parents and their peers.

There are ways of putting new life into old marriages, of putting some real romance into the status quo. We can fire up the burners of the soul to heat up cold marriages.

Some of the best marriage counseling I know came from my own bride. During one of our early conflicts, she said, "You have to work hard to stay in love." I was innocently idealistic at the time and thought, What do you mean, you have to work hard to stay in love? Love is natural. If it's really love it should not require work. Soon life made me more realistic, and I came to appreciate her words as the wisest bit of marriage counseling to be had.

The matter with many marriages is a tendency toward love laziness. Many couples become lax and unimaginative in love. Even healthy couples can allow themselves to become sexually lazy when everything isn't going just right. Many will not put the same dedicated effort into making their marriage succeed that they put into their vocation, hobby, or club.

I have a theory I share with couples who think they have fallen out of love in marriage. Men and women can love anyone of the opposite sex they choose. I believe if I should choose to love some woman other than my wife, I could love her. If my wife should choose to love a man other than me, she could do it. By the same token, if a man who has allowed his feelings to be turned off from his wife because of her peculiarities, idiosyncrasies, faults, or illnesses decides to love his wife again, he can love her as much as ever and with all the romantic feeling he ever had. The wife who has made herself indifferent to her husband so that he can't hurt her, and feels no romantic love for him, can love him as much as she could ever love any other man—if she so chooses.

All of us need to step back and take a look at our marriage. Every couple needs to think through and determine together what marriage is for them. People who don't know what they want in marriage don't know what to do with it when they get it.

The Bible has much to offer toward the understanding of marriage. Time and again, the New Testament likens the marriage relationship between husband and wife to the relationship between Christ and the church.

Back in the Old Testament, or Hebrew Testament, we learn that God made man for woman as much as woman for man. God saw that man or woman, alone, was incomplete. He created man and woman to be equal and mutual partners. They were designed and given to each other to complete and complement one another in the unique covenant relationship of marriage; there is a potent symbolism in woman's being created from the rib over Adam's heart. There is an absolute equality of woman with man. "So God created humankind in his image . . . male and female he created them" (Gen. 1:27).

Male chauvinism has always been male selfishness. This sin is now being rooted out of our culture, something which is long overdue. No marriage need stand for it.

Ephesians 5:21–33 has long been misunderstood and severely abused. Pseudo-pious men have used it as a proof text to dominate and manipulate their wives. But before it reads, "Wives, be subject to your husbands as to you are the Lord," it reads, "Be subject to one another out of reverence for Christ" (see verses 21–22). A wife's subjection to her husband is not unconditional, anymore than her subjection to the Lord. Her subjection to her husband is conditioned by the fact that he, unlike Christ, is sinful and fallible like herself.

Subjection is mutual. Many a marriage has been wrecked because a wife isn't willing to sacrifice her own work to further her husband's choice of vocation or geographical location. By the same token, many a marriage has been wrecked because a husband will not sacrifice playing golf, drinking with the fellows after work, or all-out giving to a job in order to help his wife in the kitchen, the laundry room, or the nursery.

Mutual subjection is inseparable from true love. So the scripture goes on to say, "Husbands, love your wives, just as Christ loved the church and gave himself up for her. . . . Husbands should love their wives as they do their own bodies" (Eph. 5:25, 28).

A man is to love his wife as Christ loved the church and gave himself for the church. It must not be a selfish love. Some men only show affection in the kitchen when they want some pleasure for themselves in the bedroom! Christ loved the church, not that the church might do things for him but that he would do things for the church. If the husband is head of the wife, as the apostle suggests, he must love his wife to the extent Christ loved the church—not with a love that exercises tyranny of control but with a love that is ready to make any sacrifice for her good.

Paul speaks of the marriage relationship as being "in

the Lord." That is the uniqueness of the Christian marriage. There are not just two partners but three—and the third is Christ. You may remember the archbishop at the wedding of Diana and the Prince of Wales, viewed on television, saying, "The ever-living Christ is here to bless you; the nearer you keep to him, the nearer you will be to one another."

Most running-down-and-running-out marriages are the result of a spiritual withdrawal from God and the church. When we allow ourselves to drift apart from the God who brought us together as partners, we drift apart from each other. "Unless the Lord builds the house, those who build it labor in vain" (Ps. 127:1). When we are spiritually tuned up, love is turned on.

In the light of the biblical thesis of marriage, let us consider seven day-to-day things every husband and wife can do to heat up cooling marriages.

First, we need to work harder at staying romantically in love. Don't become lazy because passion seems to be gone. Discipline yourself to act toward your partner as if you did feel love. If this sounds like hypocrisy, it is a righteous hypocrisy! Right actions will restore right feelings double-fold. Don't wait until you feel loving before doing what love would do or you will fail. Don't wait until your partner is particularly lovable before you act toward him or her as love would act. The most important thing about marriage is not having found the ideal partner but in being the best partner yourself. Ask yourself, What changes do I need to make in me to be the best partner for this person?

Second, we must work harder at good communication. No marriage relationship is any better from one moment to the next than the openness and honesty of the communication between partners. Typically, a husband will tend to react passively to pacify his spouse. Both partners need to keep each other secure enough in love that neither fears a healthy battle. Fight fairly. No hitting below the belt. Be sure to stick to the issue and don't pick on each other. Don't be afraid of differences. No difference may mean indifference, and nothing kills romance like indifference. Stay in the ring and scrap it out until the issue is resolved and both partners win a better marriage. While it may be true that the couple who prays together will stay together, it is also true that the couple that scraps together fairly will stay together happily.

Third, we need to work sensitively in giving recognition to our partner. Every person has to have "strokes" or credits. When not feeling the best toward a partner, we tend not to give commendations. Chances are, when we don't give praise we don't get praise. Two partners can starve each other emotionally for want of any recognition. Every day, look for some particular thing in your partner that you can appreciate and put your thanks into words.

Lots of sick marriages have been reborn into exciting romances overnight by a partner recognizing his or her mate with a "warm fuzzy."

Fourth, we must work at being unselfish. Unselfishness does not come naturally to most of us. We tend toward selfishness and must work hard to overcome it. Strive to be more concerned about loving than being loved. Strive to be more concerned about understanding than being understood. Swallow your pride when there has been a conflict and see if you can't beat your partner at starting a move toward reconciliation.

Fifth, we must work sensitively and thoughtfully at our God-given sexuality. Even if your body may not sense the need for such intimacy, the soul needs it and the relationship craves it. God designed us male and female so that we might have a physical means of expressing our deepest spiritual feelings. That is something far better than he has given us to express our spiritual relationship with him. By the sex drive, two partners in covenant keep being reattracted to each other in spite of all kinds of distractions: work, finances, children, weather, environment, moods, and fatigue. Every time when, amid the heavy and stressful responsibilities of the home, husband and wife are reattracted to each other and give themselves to each other, miracles happen. If one partner has done wrong, it makes forgiveness easier. It often restores broken-down communication. It covers up all kinds of faults, renews the marriage commitment, and makes incarnate the very love of God in two hearts.

Sixth, we must work hard at forgiveness. If there is anything you should forgive in your partner, for Christ's sake forgive. Forgive even "seventy times seven." Forgive as many times as the partner needs forgiveness and as many times as you need to forgive. Many couples could have the best years of their marriage yet if only one would forgive the other. If there is no sin God is willing to forgive and remove, is there any evil in our partner we dare not forgive? Nothing redeems a worn marriage like forgiveness. Until there is forgiveness there is no chance for trust to be reestablished. Some of the most beautiful marriages known have survived even infidelity, believe it or not.

Seventh, we must work at making exclusive time just for our partner. Be more creative in your time management and in finding things you can enjoy together. Nothing satisfies a woman more than to believe her husband is concentrating exclusively on her. Nothing is more gratifying to a husband than to think his wife has nothing in mind at times but him. Have you not noticed how those couple of days away from everything with your partner are always extra romantic? Work at being interesting enough to absorb your partner completely several times a week.

There is no marriage that cannot be better. There is no marriage that cannot be reborn with a little concerted effort. Think of God's kind of love—patient, kindly, thoughtful, constructive, trusting, never insisting on its own way, refusing to let itself be easily provoked—and love your partner the same way. You can put new life and exciting romance into your marriage with results beyond your wildest dreams.

14

Managing Our Grief and Helping Others with Theirs

*E*very one of us who knows love is going to know grief. Soon or late, those who love are going to be needed to help others who grieve. To get more life out of living, we must deal with the reality of death.

The time to learn how to manage grief is before it strikes. A Scottish preacher tells of an awful night in Scotland when the snow was deep and the wind shrieked around a little house in which a Presbyterian elder of the kirk lay dying. His daughter brought the family Bible to his bedside. "Father," she said, "shall I read a chapter to you?" But the elder was in sore pain and only moaned. She opened the book and began to read, until she heard him say, "No, no, lassie, the storm's up noo; I thatched ma house in the calm weather."

Once grief has struck is not the time to reason it out or hand out explanations. When grief grips us we can't hear carefully thought-out advice. It is wise to thatch the house before the storm arises. While we may not like to think of it, the storms of grief will rage around us all and around friends who need our support.

Grief is as old as love and humankind. Four thousand years ago, one anthropologist tells us, on a sunny afternoon in Egypt, heartbroken parents laid to rest in a carved sarcophagus the body of their beloved little girl. Several years ago two explorers found the tomb. They entered the cave that had been shut up all that time and found the sarcophagus. On it were inscribed the words, *O my life, my love, my little one; would God I had died for thee!* The explorers uncovered their heads reverently, left the darkness of the cave, and sealed it again, leaving love and death to their eternal vigil. How old a thing is grief! How wise it is to come to terms with it.

No matter how well informed we may be about grief management, and how prepared we may think ourselves to be, the death of a loved one hits us like a bolt of lightning. Pain seems to come from nowhere and from everywhere. Usually the initial shock is so dramatic it is difficult to think, and the electrical network of our feelings is all crossed up and shorted out. When such a time comes, don't blame yourself for having the feelings that come to you. They are normal. Don't expect to be able to control them, even though you have prided yourself on always being in control. These emotions are you, and they cannot be avoided or ignored.

Managing Our Grief

One of the best ways to ready ourselves for the inevitable griefs that are bound to come to us is learning how to help others when they are grief stricken. One of the best therapies is helping another who grieves.

At first the grieving person may appear to be accepting the death strongly and bravely. This may be attributed to shock. The shock reaction actually saves a person from having to face unbearable reality all at once. Usually this is a temporary state and the person is going to need help when the shock wears off, usually in an hour or so.

If not at once, usually soon comes a flood of tears or sobbing. Don't ever tell an adult or a child not to cry. Crying serves as a healthy relief. Because you may feel distressed by a grieving person's crying is no reason to interfere with what that person needs to do. Boys and men need special reassurance that it is all right to cry. Tear glands may be the safety valves that keep the human heart from breaking.

Dr. Erick Linderman, the former chief psychiatrist at Massachusetts General Hospital and a pioneer in the investigation of repressed sorrow, tells of a young nurse who tended her father through a long illness. She was very fond of her father and always fought back tears as she nursed him. When he died, a well-meaning but misguided friend persuaded her not to show her grief for the sake of her mother, who had a weak heart. Within hours the emotionally repressed nurse developed a case of ulcerated colitis. She corroded inwardly and eventually died, killed by the suppressed grief she would not allow herself to express. There are more people than this world knows who become chronically ill due to repressed grief locked up inside that never gets out.

Through openly vented grief we may come to grips intelligently with the cause. Who was it who said, "He washed my eyes with tears that I might see"? Don't shut down a friend's tears because you can't stand to see the friend cry. You may help yourself in doing so, but you hurt your friend.

Two things we want to avoid in dealing with grief are resentment and self-pity. One of the deadliest poisons of the human soul is resentment. "What have I ever done to deserve this? How could he leave me at this stage of my life?" Resentment is an emotional poison to the mind and, through the mind, to the body. It is known that resentment or anger harbored in the mind is a bad reaction to grief and is capable of causing physical illness. We may need to encourage a grieving friend to verbalize resentment in order to deal with the loss.

Normal grief is not self-pity, but the mistreatment of normal grief may result in self-pity. To go around feeling sorry for yourself only makes the grief more painful and destructive. The Christian needs to stop and consider how it is with the loved one in that new state of life instead of how awful it is with us now. Just think, that person is a joint heir with Jesus Christ and has inherited all that belongs to Christ!

It is very important to respect the grieving person's mood. To belittle the grieving person's feelings comes off as a put-down. To tell a person "Buck up" or "Don't cry" or "You shouldn't be angry" may cause that friend to suppress feelings that need release for the cleansing of the soul. We never want to belittle anyone's loss, even if it is a child who is grieving.

A little girl picked up the pieces of a dearly loved doll that had been dropped by a careless person cleaning her bedroom. The child was brokenhearted. The cleaning woman, irritated by the fuss the child was making, said, "Don't cry. It isn't that terrible. You'll get over it. They'll get you another one." It did matter, and everybody who understands a child's heart knows that it mattered. It was a thoughtless, even a vulgar, thing to say, like saying to a young mother who has just lost a child, "You're young; you can have more children." Of course the sorrow will pass. But it will take time. When grief comes to any one of us, in many ways we become a child again, and to help one's grieving one needs comfort and sympathy and love, not belittlement.

One of the best ways to help is to be a good listener, no matter how uncomfortable you are or how much you may disagree with what is being said. Even if the grieving are talking about how they would like to die or blaming themselves for one thing or another, extend your courtesy by letting them talk these things out of their system without interruption. Let them tell you what they are feeling and don't try to tell them what they ought to feel. You may best help them bear their burden without saying a word. A good listener is the best grief therapist. In *Macbeth,* Shakespeare offers sound counsel:

> Give sorrow words; the grief that does not speak
> Whispers the o'er-fraught heart and bids it break.

When sharing a person's early grief, don't try to theologize or say profound things; that comes later. The helper who doesn't know what to say and only offers silent embrace is of far greater help than the one who says the wrong thing. Don't tell the grieving person to accept God's will or say that God must have better things for the loved one. No grief that befalls a person is the will of God. The idea that God intends a parent to lose a child or a spouse to lose a partner is a heresy of the worst kind. In a time of grief we must not try to find solace in a false thought that makes God into a devil!

It is most important not to attempt to take over and possess the grieving person. Some very well-meaning but terribly uninformed persons will move in on the grieving person and attempt to do too much. Be sensitive and try to discern what would be helpful, leaving the grieving person free to do as much as possible for himself or herself. To deprive persons of doing what they want to do themselves, or need to be doing for themselves, can be very detrimental. The more the grieving person can do, the more the person comes to grips with reality. Strange as it may sound, having to go to the funeral home and make arrangements, pick up persons at the airport, make phone calls to relatives, and tend to details are therapeutic. Don't make a grieving person a helpless cripple out of your need to deal with your own grief.

Jesus said, "Blessed are those who mourn, for they will be comforted." J. B. Phillips translates that beatitude as "How happy are those who know what sorrow means, for they will be given courage and comfort!" (Matt. 5:4). When grieving we seem the most open to God. More than any other experience in life, grief brings us into the most intimate touch with God, when he gives us all kinds of courage and comfort. In times of grief, the Holy Spirit seems to stir up that gift of faith in which we have been nurtured.

It was prophesied of Jesus long before his birth in Bethlehem that he would be much aquainted with grief and would be sent "to bind up the brokenhearted" (Isa. 61:1).

In "Come, Ye Disconsolate," Thomas Moore wrote, "Earth has no sorrow heaven cannot heal." Nowhere does the Bible tell us not to grieve, only that we "not grieve as others do who have no hope" (1 Thess. 4:13). Grief causes great stress, but we need not let it become distress. Jesus

said that, rather than allowing ourselves to become distressed, we must hold on to our faith in God.

By faith we must look our grief straight in the face like
Jeremiah and say, "This is a grief and I must bear it" (Jer.
10:19, KJV). We must accept our grief as our share of the sorrow of the world, a sorrow that God himself eternally
shares. If we had no capacity for sorrow, it would mean we
had no capacity for love. Grief is always the evidence of
love. There is a peculiar sacredness to grief.

When grief comes our way, we must face up to it and
ask, "How can I convert this loss into a gain? How can I
turn this debt into an asset? How can I make this grief of
mine serve God's purpose in my life?"

Believe me, grief can be made to serve God. Maybe it
makes us more sympathetic with others. It may break our
self-pride. It may make us wiser in our advice when another calls upon us. In a number of ways one's grief can be
woven into the purposes of God. It is up to what, by the
grace of God, we are determined to make of it. Even the
cross was willed by wicked men, but God wove it into the
redemption of the world. Your thorns can become a
crown!

In grief we must let our faith help us. After all, we have
a hope in Christ that goes beyond this present life. This
hope is what enables us to face our own death and deal
with the death of loved ones. If you have not been involved
much in the fellowship and mission of the church, get with

it. You may find a grief support group is just what you need.

In helping others bear their grief, share your faith when the time seems right. Notice I said "share," not "evangelize." I cringe when I see religionists take advantage of grieving persons to manipulate them in a religious way.

There are times to hang on and times to let go. Letting go of something precious to us is the hardest thing in the world to do. Only God can give us the grace to let go when we must.

When Jesus told his friends of his forthcoming death, he said, "You will have pain, but your pain will turn to joy. . . . Your hearts will rejoice, and no one will take your joy from you. . . . Ask and you will receive, that your joy may be full" (John 16:20, 22, 24).

In the midst of insufferable grief we need to remember that God can work good out of everything with those who love and trust him. I remember hearing of a certain minister who carried with him a bookmark that a woman had embroidered for him. When visiting a grieving person who would be confused and unable to see how God could make any good come out of so painful a circumstance, he would show the back side, an apparently senseless mass of threads going every which way. But turned over to the right side, the thread spelled out clearly, God is love. When we can help others know the love God has for them, they will become better, not bitter, by way of their grief. So long as we can believe in God's love for us in the midst of life's most painful circumstances, we can manage our grief. Within three months one should be on the way to recovery, making reasonable decisions, getting back into life full swing, managing the inevitable setbacks, and thriving on the love of God. Thanks be to God!

15

The Best Is Yet to Be

You are going to die. So are your spouse, your parents, your children, and every one of your friends. It may happen tomorrow, or not for some years. Death may come quickly and easily, or slowly and painfully. But every one of us will, at some moment, be pronounced dead.

We may try to fool ourselves and other people. Women may dress like college coeds, learn the latest dance steps, spend a small fortune on age-defying cosmetics or cosmetic surgery and other cover-ups of age. Men may sit in front of the television set, dreaming they are still young athletes, use Grecian Formula to dye their graying hair, jog miles, and pump iron to look macho. But no matter how we try to fool ourselves, we can't bring it off. We are all getting older, and every day we are one day nearer death.

Ours is not only a cosmetic-obsessed society, ours is a health-obsessed society. We think our mortality should be under our control. We think that death is essentially a mistake and can be corrected with enough money for health insurance and ingenious medical research. We seem to think there is no reason for death, not even accidents or old age. We put health care at the top of our domestic priority list, ahead of jobs and education. Ours is such a health-obsessed society we don't know what to do with death, except to do our best to try to control and postpone it.

If any people should be able to accept their own mortality, it should be Christians. If we don't have the nerve to face up to death, we will not face up to life. Those who are prepared to live are prepared to die. Those afraid of life are afraid of death.

The old biblical character Job, having been plagued with one tragedy after another until his earthly life had become almost more than he could bear, asked the question every person asks sometime: "If mortals die, will they live again?" (Job 14:14). Job wasn't sure he wanted to live again. He had no desire to repeat the same chaotic suffering that had been his lot here on earth. Death appealed to him as a possible escape from this life's ills. But if he were to die and leave his woes behind, and enter into a new life in which God would deal kindly with him, he was ready and would welcome that.

Why should we believe in life everlasting, a far better life to be? Apart from the Bible, our sense of justice demands it. Life is grounded on moral foundations. Some things are right and some things are wrong. Right must have its reward, and wrong must exact its evil consequences. Otherwise, life is nothing but, in Shakespeare's words, "sound and fury, signifying nothing."

Within this earthly scene, we see many good people suffer, while the wicked seem to prosper. The perplexed Job complained that good persons suffer and are laughed at, and the bad persons are secure. This perplexes all of us, until we see life in the light of eternity. If death marks the end of life, the scales of justice must be out of balance. But if our life goes on, and in the next life accounting is required and righteousness gets its reward, the moral foundations are sure. The very demands of justice force us to see that everlasting life is a moral necessity.

The other reason we can believe in life everlasting is found in the Bible's teachings concerning human nature. We are not merely creatures of time and poor struggling beasts, only to lose out in the end to the infirmities of the flesh. We were made in the likeness of God. God made us for eternity, and the yearning for eternity is instinctive in us.

When preachers have said all there is to be said about everlasting life, we are still left with a hope that is uncertain. Life might be a senseless mystery and death the end of it all. But, thank God, our hope does not rest on argument. Our hope is grounded in a fact that cannot be disputed. Seeing is believing, is it not? We have seen death conquered in the resurrection of Christ. No fact in history is better documented. We are assured that those who believe in Christ are partakers in his resurrection and will inherit everything that belongs to him (read Rom. 6:5 and 8:17).

In the scripture we read that Christ died for our sins— and was buried. But that is not the whole story. He rose again the third day. In his resurrection body, Jesus was recognized by the disciples and by hundreds of others. Ask the first generation of Christians why they believed in the resurrection of the body and the life everlasting. With one voice they would answer, "Because we have seen it."

The scripture reads, "Now if the rising of Christ from the dead is the very heart of our message, how can some of you deny that there is any resurrection? . . . If Christ was not raised than neither our preaching nor your faith has any meaning at all. . . . If the dead do not rise neither did Christ rise, and if Christ did not rise your faith is futile and your sins have never been forgiven. Moreover, those who have died believing in Christ are utterly dead and gone. . . . But the glorious fact is that Christ was raised from the dead. . . . As members of Christ all . . . shall be raised to life" (1 Cor. 15:12, 14, 16–18, 20, 22, PHILLIPS).

When the Bible speaks of the resurrection of the body, it does not mean the resurrection of the flesh and bones of our present body, which are buried or cremated. Flesh and bones are not brought back together again on our resurrection day. What it means is that our personal identity is preserved and our individual personality is maintained. Can you picture any particular person without a body?

Paul likens the resurrection to the sowing of a seed in the springtime. The seed is buried in the ground and seems to die, but from it springs a whole new stock. It is not the same plant that was there before, yet the identity is definitely preserved. The scripture claims, "If there is a physical body, there is also a spiritual body" (1 Cor. 15:44).

We have no way of knowing just what this spiritual body will be like, but we do know what it is for. Our bodies are for our identity. We locate our friends because they are in identifiable bodies. So in the future life we will not be spirit ghosts, we will be real persons. Each of us will still be a separate somebody, the same person we are now. Just as we have our body now, to do what our spirit wants to do, so our ever-living spirit will have a different kind of body to do what our spirit wants to do. Just as the natural body we have now adapts us for our earthly life, so will the spiritual body that we inherit adapt us perfectly for our spiritual life.

If individual personality is to be preserved, then individual responsibility must also be preserved. The same moral distinctions that prevail here will be found on the other side. Getting to heaven depends on the same requirements as does living the best life on earth. Those who are prepared to live are always prepared to die. One world at a time is quite enough! If we live without God now, why should we expect to live with him in the world to come? Those who don't thrive on God now would probably be terribly uncomfortable with him in heaven for all the rest of their eternal life!

We can think of death as progress in whatever direction we are now heading. Those inclined toward God will rise closer to him. "And God himself shall be them" (Rev. 21:3). Those who are inclined away from God will be taken even farther away from him by death. We can only hope that God will give them another chance—and there are some biblical texts that suggest that possibility.

One of the striking facts of the New Testament account of the resurrection of our Lord is that there is no record he was ever seen after his resurrection by any unbelievers. The only ones who saw him were those who believed in him.

This is why Christians celebrate Easter. Even as Christ was raised from the dead, those who live and believe in him now shall be resurrected to live with God. Easter is our hope and belief of life beyond death, the hope of "a new heaven and a new earth," where there is righteousness and justice and where there is no more sorrow, no more suffering, no more tragedy, and no more tears. In God's presence, there is only fullness of life and joy forevermore. All this is yours if the risen Christ is the Lord of your life now.

George Bernard Shaw wrote a play about Joan of Arc, that unusual young Frenchwoman who was burnt at the stake for heresy, witchery, and sorcery in 1431 and then canonized a saint by the Roman Catholic Church in 1920. In the play, Charles VII of France is spending a sleepless night in his royal chateau. Joan was burned at the stake, the victim of Charles's stupidity and the church's foolishness. The figure of Joan becomes silhouetted against the night's lightning. Fearfully, he cries out, "Joan! Are you a ghost, Joan?" Others from a previous burning scene appear onstage, including an aging chaplain who, when he sees Joan, says, "Oh no; it was not you. . . . You are not she: Oh no: she was burned to a cinder: dead and gone, dead and gone." To this the executioner replies, "She is more alive than you, old man. Her heart would not burn; and it would not drown. I was a master at my craft . . . but I could not kill The Maid. She is up and alive everywhere."

So is it with the crucifixion of our Lord. Those Roman officers were masters at their execution craft, but they could not kill the Lord of life. His heart would not burn. He is up and alive everywhere. The promise—the hope and the possibility—is that he lives and walks in and through you and me now, this very moment.

Sydney Carter's "I Danced in the Morning," a hymn set to an old American Shaker melody, says it well:

They cut me down and I leap up high.
I am the life that will never, never die;
I'll live in you if you'll live in me;
I am the Lord of the Dance, said he.

Living in Christ, we will not know when our lives here end and our glorious new lives begin. We will be the same persons we are today, with continuity of consciousness. We will know and relate to one another again. Love will go on. Those we have loved in this world will mean far more to us than ever before. Jesus suggested that the love of heaven is so great that those who have married more than once will not have to worry about rivalries or jealousy.

For the Christian, death is the end of our sorrows, pains, and regrets—and the resurrection of our joys, health, hopes, and satisfaction.

Don't worry about your eventual death. Walt Whitman wrote, "Nothing can happen more beautiful than death." Flesh and blood cannot inherit the kingdom of heaven. Only by passing through death can you become fully alive. Believe the noted researcher in death and dying, Elisabeth Kubler Ross, when she claims, "Death is the final stage of growth in your life. It is the key to the door of life."

16

Let Go, Let God

A Christian's whole theology may be said in four words,
"Let go, let God." Most shortcomings in our life are due to
our reluctance to let go of self and let God be God. Sometimes I have an exciting time fantasizing what my life
might be like if I really let go of me and let God be God all
the way! If I were to let go of my fears and worries, I would
trust God like Job, who said, "Though He slay me, yet will
I trust him" (Job 13:15, KJV). If I were to let go of my self-
consciousness, inferiority, and depression and let God have
full sway, what confidence I could have in myself because
I trust God! If I were to let go of those concerns in my life
I perceive as being impossible, I would let God have them,
trying Jesus' promise, "What is impossible for mortals is
possible for God" (Luke 18:27). If I were to let go of the
running of my own life and let God run it, how differently
it would run. The most courageous, challenging, cheering,
and productive moments in my life have been when I
dared to let go and let Christ be my Lord.

The problem with most of us is not that we put too much over on God but that we take too much upon ourselves. The super "I" bids to be our sovereign god. In due time feelings of helplessness and hopelessness, repressed guilt, spiritual fatigue, and a yearning to escape or even to die possess us. After a while the disease progresses, and a creeping paralysis makes its way into one's soul and body, draining one's life of its energy, enthusiasm, and happiness.

The only therapy known for this common disease is a faith prescription, "Let go, let God." While this is a beautiful and provocative expression, it is a most difficult one to act out. It is so easy to say and so beautiful to ponder, but so difficult to do. We are proud and do not easily let go. We like to think we can do everything ourselves. We are determined to be in control, and to give up control is very humiliating. We are not sure we want to let go and turn over the control and destiny of our life to God. We are not sure God will want for us what we want!

We tend to let life get us down. We may experience one difficulty or disappointment after another. Any day may be a series of ups and downs, with more downs than ups. We fret about any number of problems. Our minds get to racing at top speed about unfounded fears and unreasonable things. We can't sleep, even though we are dead tired. Domestic or business pressures get to us, even to the pit of our stomachs. We manufacture more problems for ourselves. We begin to live on self-pity. We may fear we are losing our minds. We keep hanging on, trying to convince ourselves all the while that we can make it, but we are not at all sure.

One of the psalmists apparently was suffering all kinds of cares, difficulties, and troubles. He was feeling as low-down as a despairing person can get to feeling. He prayed, "Into your hand I commit my spirit . . . O Lord, faithful God" (Ps. 31:5). The psalmist was willing to surrender his own thinking, planning, will, and sovereignty and let God be God and trust his faithfulness. Here is the most daring exercise of faith, letting go and letting God. Here is the bravest prayer one can pray, "I am letting go, God, You take over." It is a prayer few among us have the faith-nerve to pray. "Lord, I put my whole being in your hands and I will keep my own hands off."

Martin Luther said the only faith that makes a Christian of us is that which casts itself on God for life or death. We may trust God too little, but we can never trust him too much.

We see that daring faith in Christ when he hung on the cross. He was repeating this psalm, "Father, into your hands I commend my spirit" (Luke 23:46). The difference between the psalmist's prayer and Jesus' prayer is that the psalmist let go and committed his life to God, confident he would escape *from* physical death; Jesus committed himself to God *in* death. Stephen repeated these same words when he was being stoned to death (Acts 7:59). He was confident that in death he was simply passing from God's earthly care to God's eternal care.

There was a man struggling with serious health problems. He said, "I care not whether I live or die. If I live God is with me, but if I die I will be with God." I don't know how many times over the years I have been with persons who were breathing their last. Some were restless and unsure about their final passage. Encouraged to let go and let God, they died a beautiful death into God's loving arms.

"Let go and let God" is not a theology for dying anymore than it is a theology for living every day. We are to put our living into God's hands as much as we are to put our dying in his care.

Of all the treasured proverbs in God's book of wisdom, none makes for more toughness of faith to me than the one in Proverbs 3:5–6, "Trust in the Lord with all your heart, and do not rely on your own insight. In all your ways acknowledge him, and he will make straight your paths." Trust God and he will direct your life.

To let go and let God does not mean to let go of our own responsibilities and them over on God. We never have the right to expect God to do anything for us that God enables us to do for ourselves. That would be "God abuse." Some think they are exercising ultimate faith when they put everything over on God and contribute no more than pious prayer verbiage.

Oliver Cromwell had a sound faith when he said to the

soldiers, "Trust in God; but . . . keep your powder dry." Always trust in God first, but don't expect him to do what you should be doing; keeping your powder dry so it will fire. To expect God's protection and providence while we do no more than pray is certainly not to honor but to tempt providence!

Augustine prayed, "O Lord, grant that I may do thy will as if it were my will; so that thou mayest do my will as if it were thy will."

While some will dismiss everything to God with a wing and a prayer, others will give up nothing to God or trust anything to him. Many have a childlike stubbornness: "I can do it myself"; "I can make it on my own"; "I can save myself from whatever I need to be saved." Some get by for years this way, priding themselves on being self-made successes. However, sooner or later that pride breaks down and they find themselves helpless. I think of one such man who has been a noted success in business and in accumulating wealth, but who is about to go blind. He has said, "I would give everything I have if God would just save my sight."

Grandparents hover over a grandchild's incubator and realize all their efforts and money are useless and there is nothing they can do except to let go and trust God to do what is best in his infinite wisdom and love. Let go and let God.

A man has malignant tumors on the liver. What can he

do about them except get the best medical attention and then let go and let God? How often the physician comes into a waiting room and announces to an anxious family, "We have done all we know to do. It is in God's hands." Only when we trust God to be in control can we be wholly at ease. Let go and let God.

To let go and let God is the same as praying what Jesus prayed, "Father, not my will, but your will be done." The question is whether we trust God's will or not. Throughout scripture we find the wise counsel to let go and let God. "Humble yourselves . . . under the mighty hand of God. . . . Cast all your anxiety on him, because he cares for you" (1 Peter 5:6–7).

A woman has a father living across the country in California who is seriously ill. She cannot leave her three small children to be with him. She asks, "How can I really let go and let God?" I suggested she take a picture she has of her father and place it on her Bible. This physical act on her part would help her realize the letting go of her father. Seeing his picture on top of the Bible might help her realize and remember that she has put him in God's care and there is nothing to frustrate her because God has him in hand.

A man is ill with a chronic condition that causes him to be overly sensitive about every little disturbance. I suggested he write down on paper the things that disturb him when they arise. Go over them with God and then burn the piece of paper, symbolizing to himself that the disturbance has been handed over to God and is out of his own hands for good.

Many among us feel guilt about things done in the past. People will hang on to these guilts, thinking that if they just suffer enough they can somehow pay their debt. It is so unnecessary to carry such burdens when Christ has already died to take those guilts from us. Until we are willing to let go of them and let Christ be our Savior, we will never be free of guilts that haunt us.

We may have developed some bad habits along the way. One man visiting me lately had gotten caught up in gambling. It was ruining his good marriage and his credit. Until he is willing to let go and let God have at his addiction, he will keep going down the drain.

Any recovering alcoholic knows that until he or she is willing to let go and let God take over, all is in vain. Those who do let go and let God take control find new life, God-broken of the demon booze.

There are persons, young and old, who are obsessed with sex. They cannot control that God-given drive and their life is all out of sorts. I have seen persons let go, cast that addiction upon the Lord, and let God be God in their life. They discover that "with God all things are possible."

If we are stubbornly determined to control all these forces in our life by ourselves, they can destroy us before we know it. Who of us can get certain resentments out of our heart until we let go and let God manage us? Who of us can control our own tongue and temper without committing them to God? Who of us can walk the valley of the shadow of death and not be afraid until we let go and let God?

Over the years I have observed that the greatest fear in people is the fear of death and judgment. Ann Landers claims the fear of death outnumbers other fears a hundred to one in letters addressed to her. Feeling there is some ultimate accounting, and knowing they are not good enough, many fear death. They are right; every one of us is "appointed once to die." There is a sure final accountability for the life God has given us. What can we do? We can only believe that "by God's grace we are saved through faith" and let go of our fear and let Christ be our Savior. Do-it-yourself salvation does not work. Try to make it on your own, make yourself perfect, and not even the death Christ died for you will do you any good.

How does one ever survive that deepest grief when a much-loved one dies? The harder one tries to forget it, ignore it, pretend it isn't for real, the more unbearable the grief grows. Sometimes people will hold on to their grief because they think that prolonged morbid grieving shows how much they loved the deceased and how they honor him or her. Jesus said, "You must not let yourselves be distressed—you must hold on to your faith in God" (John 14:1, PHILLIPS). Let go of your grief and let God deal with it, and you will find God keeps his promise, "As a mother comforts her child, so I will comfort you" (Isa. 66:13).

Oftentimes it is our ego that gives us the greatest stress. We can't get over our self-centeredness and extreme pride. We must do what is the hardest thing for us to do in this world—surrender our ego to God. Let go of ego and let God be God, and he saves us from ourselves.

We need to let go of our sins, worries, fears, illnesses, children, and our future and simply let God be the God he wants to be in our life. It is amazing what God does when he is allowed to be God in our lives. It is equally amazing what we can do when we let God be God.

I wonder how many opportunities for progress and success we miss in our lives because we will not let go and let God. I wonder how many promises of God we are missing out on because we do not let go and let God. I wonder how impoverished our lives may be because we do not let go and let God. Just imagine what God could do in your life if you would dare let go of yourself and let God be God.

What fools we be who think we can do otherwise than let go and let God be God. All I know is that when I will not let go and let God I become terribly fatigued, worried sick, disheartened, depressed, and hopeless. Could this be with you too?

Whatever your particular circumstances, I dare you to let go and let God be Almighty God in your living!